Dissertations
in
American Economic History

This is a volume in the Arno Press collection

Dissertations
in
American Economic History

Advisory Editor
Stuart Bruchey

Research Associate
Eleanor Bruchey

*See last pages of this volume
for a complete list of titles.*

THE ECONOMIC IMPACT
OF IMMIGRATION
INTO THE UNITED STATES

Peter Jensen Hill

ARNO PRESS

A New York Times Company

New York — 1975

First publication in book form, Arno Press, 1975

DISSERTATIONS IN AMERICAN ECONOMIC HISTORY
ISBN for complete set: 0-405-07252-X
See last pages of this volume for titles.

Manufactured in the United States of America

———•———

Library of Congress Cataloging in Publication Data

Hill, Peter Jensen.
    The economic impact of immigration into the
United States.

    (Dissertations in American economic history)
    Originally presented as the author's thesis,
University of Chicago, 1970.
    1. Emigration and immigration--Economic aspects--
United States. 2. United States--Emigration and
immigration--History. I. Title. II. Series.
JV6471.H54 1975   331.6'2'0973   75-2583
ISBN 0-405-07203-1

THE UNIVERSITY OF CHICAGO

THE ECONOMIC IMPACT OF IMMIGRATION

INTO THE UNITED STATES

A DISSERTATION SUBMITTED TO

THE FACULTY OF THE DIVISION OF THE SOCIAL SCIENCES

IN CANDIDACY FOR THE DEGREE OF

DOCTOR OF PHILOSOPHY

DEPARTMENT OF ECONOMICS

BY

PETER JENSEN HILL

CHICAGO, ILLINOIS

MARCH, 1970

ACKNOWLEDGMENTS

I am indebted to Professor Robert W. Fogel, my thesis chairman, for his encouragement and guidance in this thesis. His continued interest and numerous suggestions aided my work greatly. Professor Larry Sjaastad of the University of Chicago also offered helpful advice during the time of research and preparation.

Frank Hill, my brother, although reading as a non-economist, gave much assistance on one of the drafts. Finally, I also thank my wife, Lois, for her patience, understanding and encouragement during the thesis work.

TABLE OF CONTENTS

The Effect of Immigration on the People
   Already Here
Immigration and Growth, 1870-1920
Immigration and Per Capita Income
Immigration and Human Capital
Immigrant Funds and Remittances
The Effect of Differences in Age Structure
   on Savings
Immigration and Internal Migration
Economies of Scale
Summary and Conclusions

LIST OF TABLES

vii

LIST OF TABLES--Continued

CHAPTER I

THE IMAGE OF THE IMMIGRANT AS PRESENTED IN
THE HISTORICAL LITERATURE

If one accepts the views that historians hold of the immigrant, he was a boon to this country and a dire threat to its survival. The immigrant is seen as an integral element in our growth but also as a cause of economic stagnation; as a transmitter of technical information which opened up many jobs and as an unskilled laborer who threw thousands of native Americans out of work; as an addition to the labor force which allowed automation and industrialization to take place and as a fly-by-night who came only to bleed this country of its wealth before returning to his homeland; as an important carrier of capital and skills and as a tremendous burden on the welfare and law enforcement agencies of the nineteenth century. These labels and many more have been affixed to the almost 34 million people who entered the United States between 1840 and 1920.[1] Historians have long discussed the role of the immigrant in the American economy and have agreed on some issues but have had very contradictory views on others. However, even on those matters of general agreement

---

[1]United States Department of Commerce, Bureau of the Census, Historical Statistics of the United States, Colonial Times to 1957 (Washington, D.C.: Government Printing Office, 1960). Series C 133-138.

1

little or no testing of the validity of the conclusions has taken place. This thesis attempts to resolve several historical issues, particularly those relating to the economy and its performance over time. This first chapter discusses these issues as presented in the historical literature and also discusses the information necessary to test the various hypotheses.

The question that has probably raised the most discussion is how did the relative skills and abilities of the immigrant and native workers compare? This is sometimes expressed in terms of relative income positions but most often in the framework of the sort of jobs that the immigrants held in this country. Interestingly enough, almost every writer states that the immigrants were overwhelmingly unskilled when compared to the native workers, that they almost always entered the economic ladder at the bottom, and that their general economic position was much lower than that of the native born. Perhaps the strongest exponent of this belief is Oscar Handlin in The Uprooted.[1] He states:

> Wages hung close to the cost of subsistence, never rose to a point that permitted a man to accumulate the stakes of a fresh start.[2]

> The older industries had disdained the immigrants; but the new ones, high in the risks on innovation and heavy initial investments, drew eagerly on this fund of workers ready to

---

[1] Oscar Handlin, The Uprooted (New York: Grosset and Dunlap, 1951).

[2] Ibid., p. 68.

be exploited at attractively low wages.[1]

> The central condition of that lot [the lot of the immigrants]
> was inadequate earnings. Competing with each other in an
> overstocked market, the unskilled laborers forced down
> their own rate of pay. As it was lowness of wages that en-
> abled the immigrants to enter industry, the continued
> development of industry was accompanied by a steady de-
> cline in their real remuneration.[2]

> The immigrant was an exploited unskilled laborer; . . .[3]

Of course one of the basic issues here is an empirical one, and

one on which Handlin does not throw much light, namely what was the

economic position of the immigrants and how did it compare with that of

the native born? It is not clear what is meant by exploitation of the

workers; certainly wages which are low because of a low level of skills

is not exploitation in any economic sense. The author may be referring

to monopsonistic practices on the part of hiring firms, but in the com-

petitive, growing economy of the nineteenth century America, it is diffi-

cult to believe that this was a major factor in determining immigrant

wages. However, Handlin's reasoning is even more obscure when he

analyzes the reasons for the low wages. In the second quotation above he

speaks of the older industries disdaining the immigrants. This disdain

could have been the result of several causes, perhaps because of a prej-

udice on the part of the native born owners and supervisors, or even

---

[1] Ibid., p. 71.

[2] Ibid., pp. 75-76.

[3] Ibid., p. 195.

because of a dislike on the part of the older immigrants for the new immigrants. Although Handlin may be speaking in relative terms, that is, there were fewer immigrants in manufacturing than there would have been in the face of no disdain, it cannot be said that the early immigrants did not enter manufacturing. In fact, the statistics show exactly the opposite of what one might conclude from reading Handlin, as he implies that as opportunities appeared for the foreign born in manufacturing, the immigrants became more and more heavily represented in these industries relative to the native born. The censuses report that 34.4 per cent of the foreign born were in manufacturing and mechanical industries in 1870, but that by 1890 the percentage had dropped to 30.9. In the same period the native born in manufacturing and mechanical industries increased from 18.1 per cent to 19.9 per cent.[1]

Handlin's quotation, however, indicates that the disdain might have been caused not so much by prejudice as by differences in the production functions of the "new" and the "older industries." He speaks of the new ones as being risk takers and capital intensive, both factors which supposedly increase the preference for immigrants. However, a greater investment on the part of the firms would seem to make them less willing to undertake risks, particularly when compared to the less capital intensive, less automated firms that had existed earlier.

---

[1] United States Department of Commerce, Bureau of the Census, Ninth Census, 1870, I, 704, Table XXIX. Eleventh Census, 1890, Population, Part 2, p. cxlviii.

Even if the immigrants were hired in greater numbers by the newer industries, they still had inadequate earnings by Handlin's reckoning. As immigration increased over the years, possibly the supply curve of immigrant labor continually shifted downward, as Handlin implies. However, even if this were the case, the last part of the third quotation could hardly hold. The continued development of industry should have meant, at the very least, a stable demand curve and probably one that shifted upward over time. Certainly, it is difficult to see how development would lead to a lower demand curve and thus a decline in pay, unless Handlin is somehow reasoning that immigrants were only hired at low wages, and since more immigrants were hired over time, wages must have been lower.

Although other authors are not quite so convinced of the penury of the immigrants, they hold quite similar views. Maurice Davie writes that "Recent immigrant wage-earners are generally found in the lowest level of the industrial scale, receiving the pay of unskilled workmen," a condition that was not changed until the second or third generation.[1] Taft and Robbins, writing in 1955 say:

> The general effect of competition from immigrant labor was to push large numbers of native workers up into the higher semi-skilled, skilled, or white-collar occupations. The fact that so large a proportion of the rough work was done by

---

[1] Maurice R. Davie, World Immigration (New York: MacMillan Company, 1936), p. 244.

foreigners meant that it did not need to be done by the native.[1]

The National Committee on Immigration Policy takes a very similar position:

> Immigrants have tended, moreover, to take over the lowest paid and least desirable jobs in the American economy, and their coming has allowed native workers to rise in the economic scale.[2]

The quotations evidence that the immigrants have generally been regarded as unskilled whose major contribution was to release the native born from some of the more odious tasks of the society. However, even if the historians' position is correct about the almost complete lack of skills on the part of the immigrants, it does not necessarily follow that this made it possible for the native born to rise on the economic ladder. These authors seem to be suggesting a high degree of complementarity between immigrants and native born workers, a hypothesis that is made less tenable because they are usually referring to the relationship between two sets of unskilled workers, sets which one generally considers fairly close substitutes for each other. If the native workers had the requisite skills for the "higher semi-skilled, skilled, or white collar occupations," they seemingly would have been in them before the competition from the immigrants, and the presence of the immigrants would

[1] Donald R. Taft and Richard Robbins, International Migrations (New York: Ronald Press Co., 1955), p. 79.

[2] National Committee on Immigration Policy, Economic Aspects of Immigration (New York: Academy Press, 1947), p. 30.

scarcely make it easier to enter these occupations. It is an interesting theory of competition that allows some of the competitors to better their economic position in the face of increased competition. Of course, it is possible for the presence of immigrants to alter the production function to create new positions that are more remunerative for certain members of the labor force, but this can scarcely be said to be the result of "competition from immigrant labor."

Although there is considerable confusion about the way in which the immigrants entered into the economy and the channels through which they affected their own and native born earnings, the basic belief that the immigrants were unskilled, low paid workers can only be verified or disproved by empirical testing. In order to test this hypothesis, two sets of information would be useful. Of course, the most obvious would be wage information which would allow a direct comparison between the remuneration of the native and the foreign born. Without this data one could also use information about the relative skills of the two groups, such as an index of occupational distribution.

Two other issues revolve around the questions of relative skill levels and economic position, with several authors hypothesizing that skills of immigrants decreased over time and that immigrants should not have come since they did so poorly here. Through most of the literature runs the feeling that the "new" immigration, or that which came from Southern and Eastern Europe and started about 1885, was generally of a much lower skill level than the previous immigration.[1] To test this,

either wage data or skill levels would have to be available over time.

Other authors also discuss the relative economic positions of various

national groups, but not in the context of the "new" and "old" immigration.

An interesting corollary to the view that the immigrants did rela-

tively poorly in this country is that their coming was often a non-economic

response to the emotions of the time. Two recent writings on immigration

state this quite clearly:

> The movement bore in fact a distinct air of irrationality,
> even of frenzy, and many of those who took part in it were
> simply carried along by a force they did not understand.[2]

and Carlton C. Qualey states that emigrant fever affected large groups of

people and "carried hundreds and thousands along who would under nor-

mal circumstances never have left their homelands."[3]

Although I have no intentions of testing the psychological motiva-

tion of those who came to this country, knowledge of per capita incomes

in the countries of origin and in the United States would seem to throw

light on the rationality or irrationality of those who came.

---

[1]For instance see Davie, p. 239, and Jeremiah W. Jenks and
W. Jett Lauck, The Immigration Problem (6th ed., New York and London:
Funk and Wagnalls Co., 1926), pp. 198-207.

[2]Maldwyn Allen Jones, American Immigration (Chicago: University
of Chicago Press, 1960), p. 95.

[3]Carlton C. Qualey, "Immigration as a World Phenomenon," in
Immigration and American History, Essays in Honor of Theodore C.
Blegen, ed. Henry Steele Commager (Minneapolis: University of
Minnesota Press, 1961), p. 100.

Most of the concern over the immigrant skills or lack of them does not involve much detailed analysis about how these skills affected the total economy. Certainly explaining the growth of the United States in the nineteenth century is a major problem for economic historians, and it is quite plausible the immigrants played an important role in this growth. Many writers discuss this role, but few are precise in explaining just how immigrants affected economic variables, particularly the income of the native born, the per capita income of the entire economy, and the total output of the economy.

Brinley Thomas is a leading exponent of the belief that immigration was a crucial factor in the economic growth of the United States. He says:

> There is a clear positive correlation between fluctuations in immigration on the one hand and rates of change in real national income per capita and capital investment on the other. [1]

> It is reasonable to infer that each wave of immigrants (accompanied by capital imports) created conditions favorable to a high rate of capital investment, brisk industrial enterprise, the application of technical inventions, and consequently a relatively rapid increase in productivity and real income per head. [2]

> The average annual real income per head in the United States in the decade 1919-28 was $612; the corresponding figure for 1869-78 was $215. Thus in 50 years the

---

[1] Brinley Thomas, "The Positive Contribution by Immigrants; The Economic Aspect," in United States Economic History, ed. Harry Scheiber (New York: Knopf, 1964), p. 397.

[2] Ibid., p. 398.

average standard of living of the American people had risen
nearly threefold. The above analysis has shown that, in the
process of attaining this goal, the longest strides were taken
in the periods when there was heavy immigration. This correlation between a big volume of immigration and a high standard
of living also holds when we compare different regions of the
United States. In 1946 the 10 states which had the largest proportion of foreign-born also had an income of $1,344, while the
10 states which had the smallest proportion of foreign-born had
an income per head of only $739. This disparity cannot be ex-
plained by differences in natural resources or climatic conditions; in areas where immigrants have been most numerous
the pace of economic development has been most vigorous.[1]

Jones and Handlin hold similar views, with Jones stating: "Yet in
the broad view the economic effects of mass immigration were undeniably
beneficial."[2] ". . . it was the unskilled labor provided by the 'new' immigrants which alone made possible America's phenomenal industrial expansion in the late nineteenth century. . . ."[3] Handlin writes:

A completely fluid labor supply set the ideal conditions for
expansion. Thereafter, whatever branch of the economy
entered upon a period of rapid expansion did so with the aid
of the same immigrant labor supply[4]

Thus there is general agreement among many of the writers that
the immigrants were very important to economic growth. Although
Thomas reaches the same general conclusions as the other authors, he is

---

[1]Ibid., p. 398.

[2]Jones, American Immigration, p. 132.

[3]Ibid., p. 218.

[4]Handlin, The Uprooted, pp. 71-72.

more explicit in his reasons for attaching great importance to the presence of the immigrants. Nevertheless, his more detailed analysis lends
little weight to the argument that the role played by the immigrants was a
large one. A "clear positive correlation" between immigration and per
capita income changes tells us very little about cause and effect. The
strong relationship between income changes and immigration provides
just as strong support for the theory that the immigrants were pulled to
this country by desirable conditions here as for the Thomas hypothesis.
The same point holds for the correlation between state per capita income
and the proportion of foreign born in the state population.

Moreover, while it may be "reasonable to infer" that immigration
caused a "relatively rapid increase in productivity and real income per
head," it is also reasonable to infer that immigrants hardly changed productivity and per capita income at all. Thomas does not provide us with
a test capable of discriminating between these alternatives.

In order to measure the economic impact of immigration, a model
for the aggregate economy is necessary, one in which the importance of
various characteristics of the immigrant population can be identified.
Obvious ones are their skill levels and various demographic characteristics such as age and labor force participation rates.

Although the immigrants could have affected total output, they
could also have altered the per capita income of the native born. Thomas
is one of the few writers to discuss per capita income as an explicit variable, although Jones and Handlin seem to agree with Thomas' conclusion

that immigration raised income per head. However, the general tenor of much of the writing indicates that the concern over the unskilled immigrant is motivated by the belief that he lowered wages of many native workers and thus decreased incomes of much of the population. Per capita income has become an important measure of economic welfare, and the influence of the immigrant upon the income position of the native born is an important issue. There are problems in using per capita income as an index of economic well-being however, and Isaac recognizes a statistical fallacy that exists when such a measure is used over time.[1] It is possible for all non-migrants to raise their income, for all migrants to be better off, particularly if they come from a very low income country, and yet the per capita income figure for the country as a whole may be lowered. Since many immigrants to the United States came from relatively low income countries of origin, nineteenth century per capita income figures may have understated the actual economic gain that occurred.

The effect of the immigrants upon the capital of the society is discussed very little in the literature. Several attempts at measuring the amount of cash brought by entering aliens are made, but the magnitudes of the estimates are not analyzed from the viewpoint of their effect on the economy. Likewise, there is some discussion of the loss of wealth to the United States through remittances, but again no relevant measure of their

[1] Julius Isaac, Economics of Immigration (London: K. Paul, Trench, Trubner, 1947), p. 199.

importance to the economy is suggested. A more important issue is the effect of immigration on human capital. Frederich Kapp, writing in 1880, attempts to estimate the amount of human capital the United States obtained through immigration.[1] This gain is estimated at $400 million a year in 1870, but again no analysis is presented for determining the effect on the economy. Properly defining gains from increases in human capital is important, but this is not done in the literature. For instance, Brinley Thomas writes of human capital:

> Immigration provides the receiving country with a supply of labor, the cost of whose upbringing has been borne elsewhere. It is a free gift of human capital, and the smaller the proportion of dependents among the new settlers, the greater the economic advantage.[2]

The difficulty with such statements is that it is not clear who gains from such a "free gift." The residents of a country prior to immigration do not necessarily benefit from a free gift of labor, since the native born might not have had to bear the costs of upbringing even if the laborers had been raised in the receiving country. Only if certain costs of upbringing are paid for through the society, e.g., education, does a net savings result for the original members of the society. Therefore, Thomas' statement needs considerable clarification as to who reaps the "economic advantage" of which he speaks. Although the United States did receive an

[1] Frederich Kapp, Immigration and the Commissioners of Emigration (New York: Nation Press, 1880).

[2] Thomas, "The Positive Contribution by Immigrants; the Economic Aspect," p. 399.

inflow of human capital that was free in a sense, the residents of the

country did not necessarily benefit by an amount equal to the increase in

the stock of that capital.

One issue that numerous authors deal with is the influence of im-

migration upon technological change. The immigrant is often mentioned

as a carrier of technical information, but the major impact supposedly

came in a different area, the direction his presence gave to inventions

in this country. For instance, Jenks and Lauck hypothesize that:

> . . . the lack of skill and industrial training of the recent
> immigrant to the United States has stimulated the invention
> of mechanical methods and processes which might be con-
> ducted by unskilled industrial workers as a substitute for
> the skilled operatives formerly required. [1]

Brinley Thomas takes much the same position:

> One of the chief reasons why America became the home of
> mass production and the pioneer of highly mechanized pro-
> cesses was that large periodic inflows of alien labor had
> made the evolution necessary. [2]

In the last several years there has been considerable discussion

of the influence of factor prices on innovation. [3] The historical discus-

sion of technical change is imprecise, but one can place it within the

---

[1] Jenks and Lauck, The Immigration Problem, p. 198.

[2] Thomas, "The Positive Contribution by Immigrants: The Economic Aspect," p. 399.

[3] The Economic Journal, 1961 through 1966, Volumes LXXI
through LXXVI contains most of this discussion. Perhaps the best summary of the argument is contained in Syed Ahmed, "On the Theory of Induced Innovation," Economic Journal, LXXVI (June, 1966), 344-357.

recent theoretical framework developed. However, it is first necessary
to clarify what the authors mean by "mechanical methods" and "mechanized processes." One generally thinks of such inventions as raising the
capital-labor ratio, and indeed this seems to be the view taken by the
historians. Jenks and Lauck write of "mechanical methods and processes"
which served "as a substitute for the skilled operatives formerly required."
However, the recent theoretical work leads one to expect immigration to
have had an opposite effect on inventions, namely a lowering of the capital-
labor ratio. This is illustrated in Figure 1. Isoquant I represents the
production function facing the firm prior to immigration. AA is the price
line for the firm. Assume there is an Innovation Possibility Curve,
I.P.C., which is an envelope of all the alternative isoquants, each one
representing the same level of output, which the businessman thinks
could come into being with the use of the available amount of innovating
skill and time. If there is no change in the factor-price ratio, in the next
period the price line will be CC and he will choose an invention such that
he will be on an isoquant tangent to the price line, that is, isoquant III.
It should be noted that the isoquants are represented as shifting inward
with technical change in that they are unit-isoquants, representing one
unit of output.

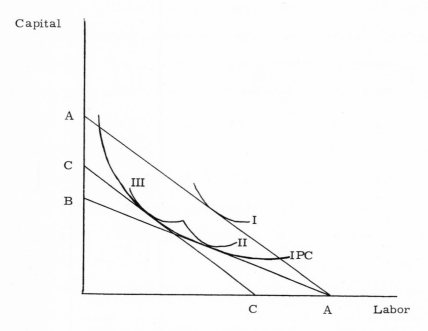

Fig. 1.--The Effect of Immigration on Invention

Assume immigration takes place which increases the supply of labor relative to the supply of capital. If there is no change in demand conditions the price of labor will fall relative to the supply of capital, as represented by price line AB. Note that the price lines AA, CC, and AB represent the relative prices of the factors, labor and capital, and not the total expenditures on the factors. If the price line is AB a different tangency to the Innovation Possibility Curve will exist than with the price line CC. Therefore the firm will choose the invention represented by isoquant II. Obviously the isoquant chosen represents a lower capital-labor ratio than III, the one that would have been chosen with constant factor prices. This is inconsistent with the conclusions reached in the literature, that immigration caused inventions which implied a higher capital-labor ratio. Whether the invention chosen is actually capital-saving or not depends upon the shape of the innovation possibility curve. Nevertheless, no matter what its shape, as long as it is convex to the origin, a lower relative wage rate means an invention will be chosen that represents a lower capital-labor ratio than would have existed with constant relative factor prices. Therefore, immigration should have meant less automation and industrialization than otherwise would have occurred.

Such analysis is open to criticism on several grounds. If immigrants brought large amounts of capital with them they could have raised the wage rate relative to the price of capital. However, evidence indicates that it is unlikely that this was the case with the nineteenth century immigration. Secondly, it is not clear that the inventions which immigrants are supposed to have induced did represent higher capital-labor ratios. From the descriptions in the literature, however, these inventions were capital using. Interestingly enough, there is little mention of the sweated industries, a labor intensive form of production which seems to have prospered during much of the era of heavy immigration. Finally, one can argue that no innovation possibility curves exist, that inventions are autonomous events with the firm not choosing between alternative inventions. If this is the case, as it may well be, it also destroys the

historical arguments about the impact of immigration, for only if choice
is involved can it be said that immigrants caused mechanical processes
and procedures to be used over other less mechanized processes.

One possibility is that the immigrant did not alter technology, but,
by changing relative factor prices, caused the firms to operate at a different point on the original production functions. A different method of combining factors does not necessarily imply technological change, although
it is often labeled such.

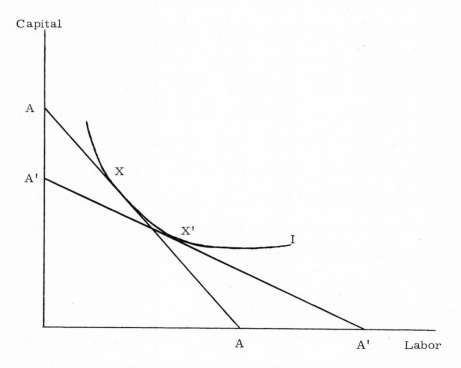

Fig. 2.--Factor Prices and Input Ratios

Figure 2 illustrates this. Assume a firm is operating on isoquant I with a price line AA. It will be producing at X, since this represents the least-cost combination of factors with the given technology. If the relative price of labor lowers, and if technology remains the same, the firm will move to X', the tangency of the new price line, A'A', to the isoquant. Although a different method of combining the factors may exist at X' compared to X, this does not represent a technological change in the pure sense. One could argue that this sort of a movement is what the authors are referring to when they speak of immigrants changing the methods of production, except for the direction of the movement along the isoquant. Again, if immigration lowered wages at all, this would imply a lower capital-labor ratio. Their writings, however, seem to indicate a substitution of capital for labor.

CHAPTER II

THE ECONOMIC IMPACT OF THE IMMIGRANTS

To resolve the questions raised in the first chapter about the immigrants and their effect on the economy some of the tools of economic analysis must be employed. There has been considerable hypothesising about the ways in which the immigrants affected the economy, and most of the hypotheses have included conclusions, implicit or explicit, about the magnitudes of such effects. This chapter deals with several of these issues and attempts to more rigorously specify and test the propositions existing in the literature.

The economic impact of the immigrant can be viewed in several ways, but when most of the writers speak of this impact, it is not clear which of the many views they are taking. In the first place, the immigrant's presence could have affected the income of the population that was present before he came. Much of the early writings arose from a fear of a worsening of the income position of the native born. Secondly, the immigrants undoubtedly had an effect on the total growth in output of the economy. The main issue here is one of magnitude; did the immigrant, because of differences between him and the native born, change the growth rate of GNP from what it would have been with a population increase from natural sources only? A third question is what happened to

20

the per capita income of the entire economy after the immigrant came? The same differences that might have affected the total output of the economy might also have altered per capita income in the country. Finally, the immigrant could have affected the economy through the capital he brought with him, both human and physical, by differences in his savings rates, through his occupational location in this country, and through economies of scale. These questions are each dealt with in sections that follow in this chapter.

The Effect of Immigration on the People Already Here [1]

Since all U.S. residents, excepting the American Indians, were present because of immigration of one period or another, we cannot, in the final analysis, speak of the effect of the immigrant on the non-immigrants. However, we can ask what the effect of the immigration during a certain time span was on those who were present at the beginning of that period. It is in this vein that the following analysis is presented.

Assume that the output of the United States can be represented by a Cobb-Douglas production function. [2]

---

[1] The analysis of this section is quite similar to that used by Harry G. Johnson, in his article "Some Economic Aspects of Brain Drain," The Pakistan Development Review, VII, No. 3 (Autumn, 1967), Mathematical Appendix I.

[2] Throughout this section of the dissertation I assume that constant returns to scale hold. This particular model does not lend itself well to consideration of increasing returns since it deals only with the short-run impact of the alteration of the capital-labor ratio. Therefore

$$(1) \qquad X = AL^{\alpha} K^{1-\alpha}$$

Assume also that the labor force is made up of two categories of workers, skilled and unskilled, and that the capital stock is composed of human and physical capital and the capital earns the same return in both forms. Then let $L = (n + N)$, n being the number of unskilled workers and N the skilled workers. Let k_1 equal the ratio of physical capital to unskilled labor and k_2 the ratio of human capital to skilled labor. Pre- and post-immigration are indicated by the subscripts 0 and 1. The marginal products of the two factors are $\frac{\partial X}{\partial L} = \alpha \frac{X}{L}$ and $\frac{\partial X}{\partial K} = (1-\alpha) \frac{X}{K}$. Therefore, prior to immigration the total output (income) is represented by:

$$(2) \qquad Y_0 = L_0 \alpha \frac{X_0}{L_0} + K_0 (1-\alpha) \frac{X_0}{K_0} = X_0$$

where $Y_0 = X_0 =$ total output (income) before immigration.

Assume that only unskilled workers immigrate and that they embody no human capital, but they do bring some physical capital with them. After this immigration the income of the original factors will be:

$$(3) \qquad Y_1 = L_0 \alpha \frac{X_1}{L_1} + K_0 (1-\alpha) \frac{X_1}{K_1}$$

---

in order to assess the long-run impact of increasing returns I present a more general discussion of the issue in a later section of the dissertation.

Assume that the immigration results in a proportionate increase of m in the number of unskilled workers and a proportionate increase of j in the material capital stock. The proportionate increase in the total labor force is represented by $\dfrac{mn_0}{n_0 + N_0}$ = a, and the proportionate increase in the capital stock is

$$\frac{jk_1 \, n_0}{k_1 n_0 + k_2 N_0} = b.$$

Therefore total output with the new immigrants and their capital present is:

(4)
$$X_1 = X_0 \, (1+a)^{\alpha} \, (1+b)^{1-\alpha}$$

where X_1 = total output after immigration, and

(5)
$$\frac{X_1}{L_1} = \frac{X_0}{L_0} \left(\frac{1+b}{1+a}\right)^{1-\alpha}$$

(6)
$$\frac{X_1}{K_1} = \frac{X_0}{K_0} \left(\frac{1+a}{1+b}\right)^{\alpha}$$

Therefore, substituting (5) and (6) into (3):

(7)
$$Y_1 = X_0 \left[\alpha \left(\frac{1+b}{1+a}\right)^{1-\alpha} + (1-\alpha)\left(\frac{1+a}{1+b}\right)^{\alpha}\right]$$

$$= Y_0 \left[\alpha \left(1 + \frac{b-a}{1+a}\right)^{1-\alpha} + (1-\alpha)\left(1 + \frac{a-b}{1+b}\right)^{\alpha}\right]$$

Approximating each of the expressions within the brackets by the first two terms of the Taylor expansion this becomes:

(8)
$$Y_1 \approx Y_0 \left[\alpha \left(1 + (1-\alpha)\frac{b-a}{1-a} \right) + (1-\alpha) \left(1 + \alpha \frac{a-b}{1+b} \right) \right]$$

$$\approx Y_0 \left[1 + \alpha (1-\alpha) \frac{b^2 - 2ab + a^2}{(1+a)(1+b)} \right]$$

$$\approx Y_0 \left[1 + \alpha (1-\alpha) \frac{(b-a)^2}{(1+a)(1+b)} \right]$$

The increase in income of the factors initially present is represented by:

(9)
$$g \approx \alpha (1-\alpha) \frac{(b-a)^2}{(1+a)(1+b)}$$

$$g \approx \alpha (1-\alpha) \frac{\left(j \dfrac{k_1 n_0}{k_1 n_0 + k_2 N_0} - m \dfrac{n_0}{N_0 + n_0} \right)^2}{\left(1 + m \dfrac{n_0}{N_0 + n_0} \right) \left(1 + j \dfrac{k_1 n_0}{k_1 n_0 + k_2 N_0} \right)}$$

Let $r_0 = \dfrac{n_0}{n_0 + N_0}$ and $k_0 = k_1/k_2$. Since $\alpha(1-\alpha)$ has a maximum value of 1/4, this may be expressed as:

(10)
$$g \leq \frac{1}{4} \frac{r_0^2 [jk_0 - m(1-r_0 + k_0 r_0)]^2}{(1+mr_0)(1-r_0 + k_0 r_0)(1-r_0 + (1+j)k_0 r_0)}$$

By using probable values for the variable in this expression one can get an idea of the magnitude of the effect of the immigrants on the income of the initial population. We shall assume that the unskilled labor is eighty per cent of the labor force ($r_0 = 0.8$), the ratio of human capital to physical capital[1] is 1/2 ($k_0 = 1/2$), and the immigration increases the

---

[1] Simon Kuznets, <u>Modern Economic Growth</u> (New Haven:

unskilled labor force by twenty per cent and the material capital by ten

per cent (m = 0.2, j = 0.1). The maximum gain in income to the original

factors is, in this case, 0.18 per cent of their original national income.

If we leave all other values the same and let j = 0, income is

increased 0.55 per cent. If we continue to let r_0 = 0.8, m = 0.2, j = 0.1,

but change k_0 to 0.75 (see footnote 1, p. 24) the increment is 0.145 per

cent. If the unskilled workers make up only sixty per cent of the labor

force (r_0 = 0.6), if the immigration increased the unskilled portion forty

per cent and the physical capital twenty per cent (m = 0.4, j = 0.2), and

k_0 = 1.33, the maximum gain in income is 0.60 per cent.[1]

It has been suggested that this model is somewhat narrow in that

it aggregates human and physical capital and does not allow the immi-

grants to bring human capital with them; that is, it assumes they are all

unskilled laborers. If one uses a Cobb-Douglas production function with

three factors of production, L, raw labor; K, physical capital; and H,

human capital, one can write:

(11) $$X = AL^{\alpha} H^{\beta} K^{\delta}$$

Yale University Press, 1966), p. 229, estimates that in 1957 the ratio of
investment in human capital to the investment in physical capital is
approximately one half. Since the ratio of human capital has probably
increased over time, a ratio of one third is also tried, but as is illustrated in the text, this alters the results very little.

[1] I am still assuming that the ratio of human capital to physical
capital is 1/2, but k_0 is changed to 1.33 by the change in r_0 from 0.8 to
0.6.

Continue to assume constant returns to scale, so that
$\alpha + \beta + \delta = 1$. The marginal products are $\frac{\partial X}{\partial L} = \alpha \frac{X}{L}$, $\frac{\partial X}{\partial H} = \beta \frac{X}{H}$, $\frac{\partial X}{\partial K} = \delta \frac{X}{K}$. Prior to immigration the income of the original factors is:

$$(12) \qquad Y_0 = L_0 \, \alpha \frac{X_0}{L_0} + H_0 \, \beta \frac{X_0}{H_0} + K_0 \, \delta \frac{X_0}{K_0} = X_0$$

No restrictions are placed on immigration this time. It can result in an increase in the amount of raw labor, human capital, and physical capital. After this immigration the income of the original factors will be:

$$(13) \qquad Y_1 = L_0 \, \alpha \frac{X_1}{L_1} + H_0 \, \beta \frac{X_1}{H_1} + K_0 \, \delta \frac{X_1}{K_1}$$

Assume that the immigration results in a p per cent increase in the raw labor force, an h per cent increase in human capital, and a k per cent increase in physical capital.

Therefore total output with the new immigrants present is:

$$(14) \qquad X_1 = X_0 \, (1+p)^{\alpha} \, (1+h)^{\beta} \, (1+k)^{\delta}$$

and

$$(15) \qquad \frac{X_1}{L_1} = \frac{X_0}{L_0} (1+p)^{\alpha-1} \, (1+h)^{\beta} \, (1+k)^{\delta}$$

(16)
$$\frac{X_1}{H_1} = \frac{X_0}{H_0} (1+p)^\alpha (1+h)^{\beta-1} (1+k)^\delta$$

(17)
$$\frac{X_1}{K_1} = \frac{X_0}{K_0} (1+p)^\alpha (1+h)^\beta (1+k)^{\delta-1}$$

Substituting (15), (16), and (17) into (13):

(18)
$$Y_1 = X_0 [\alpha(1+p)^{\alpha-1} (1+h)^\beta (1+k)^\delta + \beta(1+p)^\alpha (1+h)^{\beta-1} (1+k)^\delta$$
$$+ \delta(1+p)^\alpha (1+h)^\beta (1+k)^{\delta-1}]$$

If $\alpha = 0.6$, $\beta = 0.2$, and $\delta = 0.2$, and if the immigrants increase the raw labor by thirty per cent ($p = 0.3$), the human capital by ten per cent ($h = 0.1$), and the material capital by twenty per cent ($k = 0.2$), then one plus the change in the income of those initially present equals 1.0023. That is, immigrants increase the income of the original factors by 0.23 per cent.

If $\alpha = 0.5$, $\beta = 0.2$, $\delta = 0.3$, and if $p = 0.4$, $h = 0.2$, $k = 0.3$, their income is increased by 1.0022, or 0.22 per cent.

It is evident from these numerical examples that the use of any plausible values in these models will yield almost negligible effects on per capita income of the initial population. This is particularly true since it is only over decade intervals that the increases postulated here could hold. It should be noted though, that while these calculations indicate a very small increase in income for the total initial population, certain members of that population could also have experienced substantial

losses or gains in income due to immigration.

Immigration and Growth, 1870-1920

Another question of interest is how much various physical

characteristics of the immigrant population influenced overall growth. It

is often argued in the literature that there were three major differences

in the immigrant population that had a significant effect on economic growth

although no one author argues all three positions. It is said that (1) the

immigrants were more concentrated in the productive age groups; (2)

had higher labor force participation rates, thus raising the growth rate;

and (3) the immigrants were of a lower labor force quality. This last

factor would seem to imply a lower growth rate, but as illustrated in the

first chapter, several authors disagree, feeling that the low level of skills

hastened industrialization and growth. A model is presented below that

isolates these factors and allows an assessment of their importance. It

should be noted that this analysis focuses primarily on the physical quan-

tities of labor and capital and makes no attempt to correct them for quality

change. A partial quality adjustment factor is used in the model, λ , but

it simply represents the ratio of the index of the occupational composition

of foreign labor to the index of the occupational composition of native

labor. Therefore, the usual large residual results, which can either be

attributed to disembodied technological change (assigning it all to the A

term), or one can make quality adjustments in the inputs, which have removed almost all of this residual for modern data. No adjustments of this sort have been made for this paper. It should also be noted that this model does not include an explicit variable for the age differences in the native and foreign born. However, this is partially taken into account in the labor force participation rate variable. It is evident from Table 29, Appendix A, that participation rate differences are, for a large part, simply reflections of age differences in the two populations. Differences in the occupational mix, as measured by λ, also probably reflect age differences.

Again assume a Cobb-Douglas production function:

(19) $\quad Y = A(t) L^{\alpha} K^{1-\alpha}$

where Y = income
L = labor force
K = capital stock
α and A are technological parameters.

(20) $\quad L = \lambda L_f + L_n$

where λ = quality correction term for differences between the native born and foreign born labor force
L_n = native born labor force
L_f = foreign born labor force.

and

(21) $\quad L = \lambda \gamma_f P_f + \gamma_n P_n$

where P_f = foreign born population
P_n = native born population
γ_n = foreign labor force participation rate
γ_n = native labor force participation rate.

since

$$\gamma_f P_f \approx L_f$$

$$\gamma_n P_n \approx L_n$$

from equation (21) it can be shown that:

(22) $$L^* = \frac{\lambda L_f}{L}(\lambda^* + P_f^* + \gamma_f^*) + \frac{L_n}{L}(P_n^* + \gamma_n^*)$$

where each of the starred terms represents the percentage rate of growth of that variable. Substituting into the original production function:

(23) $$Y^* = A^* + \alpha[\lambda \frac{L_f}{L}(\lambda^* + P_f^* + \gamma_f^*) + \frac{L_n}{L}(P_n^* + \gamma_n^*)] + (1-\alpha)K^*$$

Table 1 presents the values for the variables of equation (23) from 1870 through 1920 and Table 2 presents the percentage rates of growth of these variables, which is the form in which they are used in equation (23). Of course, one of the most interesting statistics in Table 1 is λ. It indicates that the labor force quality of the foreign born was very close to that of the native born. The derivation of λ is discussed in Appendix II, and there is further discussion of the significance of these estimates in the third chapter of the thesis.

The values from Table 2 are inserted in equation (23), which then yields a measure of the contribution of the various factors to growth. In order to evaluate equation (23) assume $\alpha = .75$ and $1-\alpha = .25$. Since the foreign born population was also responsible for a portion of the

TABLE 1

POPULATION, LABOR FORCE QUALITY, AND LABOR FORCE
PARTICIPATION RATES, NATIVE AND FOREIGN
BORN, AND CAPITAL STOCK, 1870-1920[a]

Year	P_f 1000's	P_n 1000's	λ	γ_f %	γ_n %	K billion $
1870	5,567	32,991	.97	48.6	29.7	9.5 (1850)
1880	6,680	43,476	.99	52.3	32.0	45.6
1890	9,250	53,698	.95	55.2	32.8	82.1
1900	10,341	65,653	.97	57.6	35.5	117.6[c] 101.5[d]
1910	13,516	78,456	(.95)[b]	57.8	38.7	158.5 (1912)
1920	13,921	91,790	.93	55.6	36.9	218.1 (1922)

[a]Sources: P_f and P_n from U. S. Department of Commerce,
Bureau of the Census, Fourteenth Census of the United States, 1920, II,
Table 4, 30. λ, see Appendix II. γ_f and γ_n: for 1870, from U. S.
Department of Commerce, Bureau of the Census, Ninth Census of the
United States, 1870, I, Table 24, 704. 1880 from U. S. Department of
Commerce, Bureau of the Census, Tenth Census of the United States,
1880, I, Population, Table 27, 744. 1890 from U. S. Department of
Commerce, Bureau of the Census, Eleventh Census of the United States,
1890, XII, Population, Part 2, Table 82, 354-358. 1900 from U. S.
Department of Commerce, Bureau of the Census, Twelfth Census of the
United States, 1900, Special Reports, Occupations, Table 2, p. 10.
1910 and 1920 from U. S. Department of Commerce, Bureau of the
Census, Fourteenth Census of the United States, 1920, IV, Population,
Table 4, 341. K from Raymond Goldsmith, "The Growth of Reproducible
Wealth of the United States from 1805 to 1950," in Income and Wealth of
the United States, Trends and Structure, Income and Wealth, Series II
(Cambridge: Published for the International Association for Research
in Income and Wealth by Bowes and Bowes Ltd., 1952) Table 1, pp.
306-7.

TABLE 1--Continue

[b]An estimate of λ is not available for 1910, so a value halfway between the values for 1900 and 1920 is used.

[c]This estimate differs from another one for 1900, produced directly below it, but is based on the same series as the estimates for 1870, 1880, and 1890. Therefore this estimate is used in calculating the percentage rate of change from 1890 to 1900 of Table 2.

[d]This estimate is from the same series as the estimates for 1910 and 1920 and therefore has been used in calculating the percentage rate of change from 1900 to 1910 of Table 2.

TABLE 2

ANNUAL PERCENTAGE RATES OF CHANGE FOR EACH DECADE: BASED ON VALUES FROM TABLE 1

Year	P_f^* (%)	P_n^* (%)	λ^* (%)	Y_f^* (%)	Y_n^* (%)	K^* (%)
1870-1880	1.84	2.80	.20	.74	.75	5.38
1880-1890	3.31	2.13	-.40	.54	.24	6.06
1890-1900	1.12	2.03	.21	.48	.25	3.66
1900-1910	2.71	1.80	(-.20)	.03	.87	3.78
1910-1920	.29	1.58	-.20	-.37	.46	3.24

capital formation, it is necessary to assign part of K^* to them. Assume the foreign born contributed to capital formation in direct proportion to their presence in the population at the beginning of each period. K_n^* will represent the native born's growth in capital and K_f^* the foreign born's growth. The results of this model are presented in Table 3. Lines 1 through 7 of Table 3 list the contribution of each factor; labor force quality, population growth, labor force participation rates, and capital formation, to the total growth for each decade. It should be noted however, that though these figures are each for a decade, they represent the annual rate of growth within that decade. Thus the total growth that is explained by changes in the variable of lines 1 through 7 varies from a high of 3.90 per cent per year for the years 1870-1880, to a low of 1.44 per cent per year for the decade 1910-1920. Care must be exercised in the interpretation of Table 3 however. The contributions of each of the factors in lines 1 through 7 are marginal contributions in that they represent the effect of the change in that factor from the previous decade. Therefore the contribution of any one individual factor, for instance the population of the foreign born, is predicated upon the presence of the foreign born at the end of the previous decade. The table is designed to measure the importance of immigration in total growth in each decade, given the actual behavior of both the native and foreign born populations; therefore one cannot argue that if there had been no immigration for the entire period that the growth rate would have been lowered by the sum of lines 1, 2, 3, and 7.

Lines 9 through 12 allow a more complete assessment of the contribution of the foreign born to the growth in total output. Line 9

TABLE 3

THE CONTRIBUTIONS TO GROWTH BY THE NATIVE BORN AND FOREIGN
BORN POPULATIONS, 1870-1920

		1870-1880	1880-1890	1890-1900	1900-1910	1910-1920
(1)	$\alpha\lambda \dfrac{L_f}{L}\lambda^*$	.0003	-.0006	.0003	-.0003	-.0003
(2)	$\alpha\lambda \dfrac{L_f}{L}P_f^*$	.0029	.0049	.0018	.0040	.0004
(3)	$\alpha\lambda \dfrac{L_f}{L}Y_f^*$	.0012	.0008	.0008	.0000	-.0005
(4)	$\alpha \dfrac{L_n}{L}P_n^*$	.0166	.0128	.0199	.0108	.0095
(5)	$\alpha \dfrac{L_n}{L}Y_n^*$	.0044	.0014	.0015	.0052	.0028
(6)	$(1-\alpha)\dfrac{K_n}{K}K_n^*$	.0114	.0125	.0082	.0078	.0074
(7)	$(1-\alpha)\dfrac{K_f}{K}K_f^*$	.0022	.0026	.0010	.0016	.0007
(8)	Total	.0390	.0344	.0255	.0291	.0144

(9)	1 + 2 + 3 + 7	.0064	.0077	.0039	.0053	.0003
(10)	9/8	.1641	.2238	.1529	.1821	.0208
(11)	2 + 7	.0051	.0075	.0028	.0056	.0011
(12)	11/9	.797	.843[a]	.718	.949[a]	.579[a]

[a]The growth rates from 1880-1890, 1900-1910 and 1910-1920 contain negative elements. Line 12 measures the contribution of the population growth and capital formation of the foreign born to the total contribution by the foreign born (line 9). In order to make this measure more meaningful, in calculating line 12 the total change is used; that is, the negative elements are treated as positive. Otherwise, for 1900-1910 and 1910-1920, line 12 would be greater than 100 per cent. Therefore, the values for lines 8 through 11 are reported for 1880-1890, 1900-1910 and 1910-1920 are not the values used for computing line 12 for these dates.

lists the total immigrant contribution, assuming that all changes in $\lambda*$, line 1, are the result of variations in foreign born labor force quality rather than in native born quality. However, since $\lambda*$ is responsible for a very small portion of total growth, this assumption is not crucial in assessing the importance of immigrants. From line 10 it is evident that the immigrants' contribution in each decade to total growth was fairly constant for the first four decades of the period, varying from 16.4 per cent to 22.4 per cent. However, in the last decade, 1910-1920, their contribution falls considerably, to 2 per cent. This of course, is largely due to the almost complete cessation of immigration in the latter half of the decade.

Through much of the historical literature runs the feeling that a major contribution to the growth of the nineteenth century was the very high labor force participation rates of the foreign born. Table 1 shows that these rates were considerably higher for the foreign born for the entire period. The literature also embodies the hypothesis that differences in labor force quality between native and foreign born workers were also quite an important influence on growth of total output. Several of the authors feel that a supposed lack of skills aided industrialization and growth, and others indicate that this lack retarded it. In an attempt to measure just how important these supposedly crucial elements were, lines 11 and 12 are computed. Line 11 states the contribution of the two "normal" factors of the immigrant population, their population growth and their capital formation. These factors receive very little attention in the literature and would seem to be of much less importance than their labor force quality, labor force participation rates, and age differences. Line 12 measures the contribution of the growth of the foreign born population and the foreign born's capital formation to the total contribution of the foreign born (line 9). Interestingly, the population growth and capital formation were responsible for approximately three-fourths of this. It can be argued that the growth in total output varied little from what it would have been if the same amount of population and capital growth would have taken place by the native born. Needless to say, this conclusion is at variance with the hypotheses presented in the literature, where one is lead to believe that the immigrants altered growth significantly from what it would have been in the face of an identical increase in population by the native born. [1]

Immigration and Per Capita Income

The first section of this chapter analyzed the effect of immigration on the incomes of those present before any given influx of people. The mechanism through which the immigrants could have altered the income of those initially present was a change in the capital-labor ratio.

---

[1] In calculating the data for Table 3 I also used $\alpha = 0.50$ and $1-\alpha = 0.50$. Using such values alters my results very little and the direction of the effect gives even stronger support to these conclusions.

This effect was shown to be negligible since the immigrants changed incomes less than one per cent, even over periods as long as a decade. In the last section my calculations indicated that the immigrants were responsible for between 16 and 22 per cent of the growth in total output between 1870 and 1910, and that most of this was due to the physical presence of the immigrants and their capital, rather than the differences in the quality of the native and foreign born labor forces and the labor force participation rates. However, it is possible that these characteristics, the labor force quality and labor force participation rates of the foreign born, while not significantly altering the rate of growth of income, could have had an effect on the level of per capita income. This issue differs from the analysis of the first section in several ways. In the first place, one is now concerned with the level of per capita income of the entire population, not just the income of those present before immigration. Secondly, the formulation presented in this section is not based upon a production function, as is the model used in section one, and consequently does not assess the effects of changes in the amounts of the factors of production. Rather it is explicitly designed to measure the effect of the two characteristics of the foreign born population that are considered important, labor force quality and labor force participation rates. This can be seen in the following formulation:

$$(24) \quad \frac{Y}{P} = \frac{Y}{L} \, \gamma$$

where Y/P = per capita income
Y/L = income per labor force member, or labor force productivity.
γ = labor force participation rate.

also

$$(25) \quad \gamma = \frac{P_f}{P} \, \gamma_f + \frac{P_n}{P} \, \gamma_n$$

where γ = labor force participation rate of the total economy.
P_f = foreign born population.
P_n = native born population.
P = total population
γ_f = foreign born labor force participation rate.
γ_n = native born labor force participation rate.

and

$$(26) \quad \frac{Y}{L} = \frac{L_n}{L} \left(\frac{Y}{L}\right)_n + \frac{L_f}{L} \left(\frac{Y}{L}\right)_f$$

where $\frac{Y}{L}$ = labor force productivity of the total labor force.
L_n = native born labor force.
L_f = foreign born labor force
L = total labor force
$\left(\frac{Y}{L}\right)_n$ = labor force productivity of native born.
$\left(\frac{Y}{L}\right)_f$ = labor force productivity of the foreign born.

Since

$$(27) \quad \left(\frac{Y}{P}\right)_n = \left(\frac{Y}{L}\right)_n \gamma_n \, ,$$

$$(28) \qquad \frac{\frac{Y}{P}}{\left(\frac{Y}{P}\right)_n} = \frac{\frac{Y}{L}}{\left(\frac{Y}{L}\right)_n} \quad \frac{Y}{Y_n}$$

Equation (28) expresses the fact that the ratio of the actual per capita income at any given date to the per capita income that would have existed had all the population been native born (i.e., with no immigration), is equal to the ratio of the respective labor force productivities and labor force participation rates; that is, the ratio of the total labor force productivity to the native born labor force productivity, and the ratio of the total labor force participation rate to the native born labor force participation rate.

Although a measure of the individual labor force productivity of each population group is not available, the relative productivity of the foreign born labor force is represented by λ of section two of this chapter. By using these values, equation (26) yields the labor force productivity, $\frac{Y}{L}$, of the entire economy. Of course, the labor force participation rates for the native and foreign born are readily available, and the aggregate rate is calculated from equation (25). Table 4 presents the results of these calculations in the form of the ratios of equation (28). The total change in per capita income, column 3, is the result of multiplying column 1 with column 2.

The two factors have opposite effects, with the lower labor force quality of the foreign born serving to lower per capita income; and the

41

TABLE 4

THE EFFECT OF THE FOREIGN BORN ON PER CAPITA INCOME

Year	$\dfrac{Y/L}{(Y/L)_n}$	$\dfrac{Y}{Y_n}$	$\dfrac{Y/P}{(Y/P)_n}$
1870	.993	1.091	1.083
1880	.998	1.084	1.081
1890	.989	1.100	1.088
1900	.994	1.084	1.077
1910	.990	1.072	1.061
1920	.987	1.068	1.054

higher labor force participation rates of the foreign born raising per capita income. The labor force participation rate effect is by far the strongest; thus per capita income was higher because of the presence of the foreign born by 5.4 to 8.8 per cent. The interpretation of these results is not clear however. Per capita income is the most common measure of economic welfare, and one might argue that the total population had approximately a seven per cent gain in economic well-being because of the presence of the immigrants. However, using per capita income as an index of economic welfare over time can be rather misleading, particularly when family size and the age structure of the population change. In this case it can be argued that the per capita income measure is not valid because of large differences in the age structure of

the native and foreign born population. Nevertheless, this is an index
that is used frequently, and this index has been measurably changed by
the presence of the immigrants.

A more basic problem with the data of Table 4, however, is that
the labor force participation rates of the native born, which are used in
the denominator in calculating column 2, are not representative of those
that would have existed in the absence of immigrants. This fact exists
because many children of immigrant families were born in this country
and, therefore, are included in the native born statistics. Their presence biases the native population strongly towards the younger ages and
creates a relatively low labor force participation rate on the part of all
native born. In an effort to remove this bias I have recalculated the
statistics of Table 4, making two adjustments. I have used as the native
born population the native born white of native parents and the total
colored population, of which almost all was native born of native parents.
I have also calculated these statistics on the population ten years old and
over, thus removing a large portion of the children from both the native
and foreign born population. Since productivity figures are not available
for the native born of native parents I have assumed that the ratios used
in column 1 of Table 4 still apply. In this case the data is available only
for 1890 through 1920.

In this case per capita income is raised by the immigrants, but
not nearly as much as under previous assumptions. It should also be

TABLE 5

THE EFFECT OF THE FOREIGN BORN ON PER CAPITA INCOME, ADJUSTED

Year	$\dfrac{Y/L}{(Y/L)_n}$	$\dfrac{Y}{Y_n}$	$\dfrac{Y/P}{(Y/P)_n}$
1890	.989	1.050	1.038
1900	.994	1.029	1.023
1910	.990	1.021	1.011
1920	.987	1.034	1.021

noted that the figures of column 3 represent the increase in the per capita income of the population 10 years of age and older, not the entire population. Since this last table is probably a more accurate representation of the actual increase in per capita income that resulted from immigration than Table 4, again one concludes that the economic impact of the immigrants was not large.

Immigration and Human Capital

Although the importance of human capital in economic growth has been emphasized a great deal in the last several years, it was recognized as an important issue in evaluating the effects of immigration much earlier. Frederich Kapp, writing in 1880, attempted to estimate

the capital value of immigrants. [1] Several more attempts followed this,
but none adequately defined how the increase of human capital through
immigration affected this country. It is evident that such an increase
would result in an increase in total output, but the owners of the human
capital, namely the immigrants, would, in the absence of externalities
and non-constant returns to scale, capture the return on this capital,
thus leaving the rest of the economy unaffected. It has also been shown
in the first section of this chapter that the effect of the immigrants and
their capital on the income of those already here through alterations of
the capital-labor ratio would have been negligible.

However, insofar as the investment in human capital is carried
out by others than the individual himself, a net gain or loss could result.
The major area that comes to mind is education, where a large portion
of the cost is borne by taxpayers. This can perhaps best be viewed as
an intergenerational transfer of resources whereby one generation is
educated and then, when it becomes of productive age, is expected to pay
for the next generation's education. In the case of immigrants one part
of this transfer is missing in that the productive foreign born were expected to pay for the next generation's education but did not receive
their education in the United States. Therefore, the education bill, both
public and private, was lower at any given date because a portion of the

[1] Frederich Kapp, Immigration and the Commissioners of
Emigration (New York: Nation Press, 1880).

population received its education abroad. One can measure this effect by asking the counterfactual question, given the population that actually existed in the United States, what would education costs have been if all members of this population would have been native born, i.e., educated in the United States?

Such a calculation is made for 1880, but it is carried out only for elementary education. This takes into account almost all of the effect of immigrants on the total educational bill, since in 1880 public elementary school costs were 97 per cent of the direct expenses for public elementary and secondary schools.[1]

In order to determine how many more elementary age people there would have been if all immigrants would have been native born, I have used the age structure of entering immigrants.[2] For the period 1880 through 1898 there are three categories, 0-15, 14-40, and 41+. After 1891 the last category becomes 45 and older. I have used the ages 7 through 14 for the period of elementary schooling. In order to determine the number of immigrants who would have been in school in 1880, I have calculated the number entering in each year who would have been

---

[1] Lewis C. Solmon, "Capital Formation by Expenditures on Formal Education, 1880 and 1890" (unpublished Ph.D. dissertation, University of Chicago, 1968), Table 7, p. 49.

[2] U. S. Department of Commerce, Bureau of the Census, Historical Statistics of the United States, Colonial Times to 1957 (Washington, D. C.: Government Printing Office, 1960), Series C 133-138.

between the ages of 7 and 14 in 1880. For instance, in 1884 those entering the United States who were between the ages of 11 and 18 would have
been of school age in 1880. In order to calculate the number of school
age in 1880, I have assumed that the entrants in the first two age categories, 0-14, and 15-40, are evenly distributed among all ages in each
category. For instance, of those entering between the ages of 15 and 40,
1/26th, or 3.85 per cent would have been 30 years old.

Of those who immigrated from 1881 through 1898, there would
have been 1,657,253 of school age in 1880. However, there were also
departures of foreign born during this period. Kuznets and Rubin estimate that between 1878 and 1897 departures were 25.4 per cent of
arrivals.[1] I have assumed that the age structure of those departing was
the same as that of the arrivals, therefore I have decreased the number
of school age immigrants 25.4 per cent, to 1,236,310. The same sort
of calculations are applied to later periods. Between 1899 and 1910 I
have used Kuznets and Rubin's departure ratio of 47.1 per cent, which
is estimated for the period 1897 through 1918. Starting in 1911 I have
used more precise departure statistics which are available for each
year.[2]

---

[1] Simon Kuznets and Ernest Rubin, Immigration and the Foreign
Born (National Bureau of Economic Research Occasional Paper 46; New
York: National Bureau of Economic Research, 1954), p. 22.

[2] Ibid., p. 96.

Although the assumption that the immigrants were evenly distributed among all ages in the first two age groups probably does not violate
reality very much, the same sort of assumption cannot be made for the
immigrants in the last category, 45 years and older. Therefore, I have
examined the age structure of the entire population in 1910 and attempted
to apply these statistics to the entering population. Thus I have assumed
65 per cent of the entering immigrants 45 and older were between the
ages of 45 and 59 and the rest were between 60 and 74. In 1910 actually
94 per cent of those 45 and older were between the ages of 45-74. I have
also assumed that within these two categories, 45-59, and 60-74, the
immigrants were evenly distributed among all ages.

One other adjustment was necessary in my calculations, since
between 1932 and 1935 there was net emigration from the United States.
Therefore I have used the net immigration from 1932 through 1940 and
applied the age statistics to this figure to calculate the number of school
age children in 1880. Although my calculations continue through the 1940
enumeration of entering immigrants, it is interesting to note that of the
total number of immigrants who would have been in school in 1880, 80.2
per cent entered between 1881 and 1910 and 96 per cent entered between
1881 and 1917.

The total number entering who would have been of school age in
1880 is 2,889,367. The census data on school attendance indicates that

approximately 85 per cent of this age group was in school.[1]   Applying

this statistic to the school age entering immigrants this yields a figure of

2,455,962. Solmon[2] lists total public school attendance (elementary and

secondary) in 1880 as 9,703,399. He also gives the percentage of public

urban school enrollment which was high school enrollment, allowing one

to calculate the number of elementary school pupils, 9,631,962. Solmon

also calculates the private elementary school costs per pupil as being 1.3

times the public elementary costs per pupil. If one divides the private

elementary costs by 1.3 this gives a result I term the adjusted private

elementary costs. The sum of the adjusted private elementary costs and

the public elementary costs divided into the adjusted private elementary

costs yields a figure of 8.22 per cent. Thus, I have assumed that 8.22

per cent of the total elementary school enrollment is private and have

applied this figure to my estimate of the school age children of foreign

birth, giving a public elementary figure of 2,254,082. This is 24.2 per

cent of the actual public elementary enrollment in 1880, so the costs of

public education and the enrollment would have been almost one quarter

greater if the United States would have had to educate all of her population.

---

[1]U. S. Department of Commerce, Bureau of the Census, Eleventh Census of the United States, 1890, Compendium, 3, p. 268, and U. S. Department of Commerce, Bureau of the Census, Fourteenth Census of the United States, 1920, II, 1044, Table 2.

[2]Solmon, "Capital Formation by Expenditures on Formal Education 1880 and 1890," p. 108, Table 23.

Consequently, the American taxpayer enjoyed a considerable windfall through not having to educate her entire population.

Although there was considerable savings in the form of less education costs, this savings did not result in a large scale reduction in total government spending. Estimates of state and local expenditures are not available for 1880. However, they are available for 1890, and an estimate can be made for 1880 from the 1890 data.[1] The receipts from ad valorem taxes are given for 1880 and 1890. In 1890 they were 75.8 per cent of state and local receipts, and it is assumed that this figure also applies to 1880. In 1890 expenditures were 97.3 per cent of total receipts, and if this also applies in 1880, total state and local expenditures were 401.5 million. Federal government spending was 268 million dollars in 1890.[2] If we assume that educating all the foreign born would have increased high school costs by the same proportion that it increased elementary school costs, 24.2 per cent, the total government spending bill would have been 3.45 per cent higher if the immigrants had been educated here, and the state and local spending would have been 6.00 per cent higher. Most of this increase is because of the increased number of elementary pupils, since the state and local spending would have been 5.00

---

[1] 1880: U.S. Department of Commerce, Bureau of the Census, Tenth Census of the United States, 1880, VII, 18. 1890: U.S. Department of Commerce, Bureau of the Census, Eleventh Census of the United States, 1890, XV, Part 2, 417.

[2] U. S. Department of Commerce, Bureau of the Census, Historical Statistics of the United States, Colonial Times to 1957 (Washington, D. C.: Government Printing Office, 1960), p. 711.

per cent greater if the foreign born had only received an elementary education here.

Another measure of the effect on the United States of this "free" human capital can be obtained if we approach the figures from the aggregate level. If we assume that the U. S. residents of 1880 allocated a certain portion of total output to capital formation, both human and physical, the fact that they had to invest less in education, or human capital formation, meant that physical capital formation was greater. In this case I estimated what the total cost increase of elementary education would have been, for both private and public schools. Using Solmon's figures[1] I have calculated an educational cost of $9.69 per elementary pupil in 1880. He estimates private elementary costs as 1.3 times public costs, but this estimate does not include costs of boarding rural teachers. Therefore, I have multiplied 1.3 times $8.58, the cost per public elementary pupil excluding board for rural teachers, to arrive at a figure of $11.15 per private elementary pupil. My calculations indicate that there would have been 201,880 more private elementary pupils and 2,254,082 more public elementary pupils had the immigrants been educated in the United States. This yields an increase in the cost of education of $24,093,017. In 1880 gross capital formation was 1.65 billion

---

[1] Solmon, "Capital Formation by Expenditures on Formal Education, 1880 and 1890." Tables 23, 24, and 7.

dollars.[1] If this figure was greater by $24 million dollars because of a savings in educational costs, gross capital formation was 1.5 per cent higher as a result of this savings.

Obviously the fact that the United States did not have to educate a fairly large portion of her population resulted in a considerable gain in that educational costs were lower. However, it does not seem that this gain was so large as to have made for a much lower tax bill for the average U.S. citizen, nor does it seem to have aided capital formation and growth significantly.

Immigrant Funds and Remittances

The historical literature has given a fairly large measure of consideration to the questions of the amount of funds entering immigrants brought with them and the amount of remittances that were returned to their home countries. The first has been claimed as a major source of capital and the latter as a major loss to the economy. In every year after 1872 remittances were greater than funds brought so there was a net loss to the economy for most of the latter part of the immigration period. In order to put these claims in perspective, several dates have been chosen from the immigration period. The net movement of funds (remittances

---

[1]Robert Gallman, "Gross National Product in the United States, 1834-1909," Output, Employment, and Productivity in the United States after 1800 (Studies in Income and Wealth, Vol. XXX, Confrernce on Research in Income and Wealth; New York: National Bureau of Economic Research, 1966), p. 34.

minus funds brought) is available for each of these dates and these
figures are compared with total income and gross capital formation for
those dates. The results are presented in Table 6 below. Although the
importance of remittances and funds was increasing over time, it nevertheless does not appear that they were as crucial as supposed by several
writers.

TABLE 6

IMMIGRANT FUNDS AND REMITTANCES[a]

Year	net outflow (million dollars)	% of national income	% of gross capital formation
1880	4	0.05	0.24
1890	45	0.42	1.70
1900	90	0.60	2.83
1910	204	0.71	

[a]Sources: net outflow: Historical Statistics, Series U 183, pp.
564-565. National Income: Ibid. Series F 1 and Series F 7, p. 139. I
have assumed for the dates prior to 1900 that national income was 85 per
cent of GNP. Gross capital formation: Gallman, "Gross National Product
in the United States, 1834-1909," p. 34, Table 21.

The Effect of Differences in Age Structures on Savings

The previous sections of this chapter have dealt with questions
that have arisen in discussions of the immigrant in the historical literature. However, one issue is of importance that has received almost no

consideration by the historical writers. Modern economists have suggested that demographic differences in population can sharply influence
growth, with a major area of this impact being in savings rates. This
same hypothesis applies to the nineteenth century United States, where
there were large-scale differences in the age structure of the native and
foreign born populations, as is evident from Table 22, Appendix A. The
suggestion has often been made that these age differences sharply affected
growth through labor force participation rates, and this hypothesis is
tested in section two of this chapter. My results show that this impact
was not large. However, the possibility that the age differences were
felt in another way, through their influence on savings rates, has often
been overlooked. This section tests the hypothesis that these differences
changed the overall savings rate enough to seriously affect growth. An
empirical estimate of the life cycle of savings is applied to the population
at decade intervals in an attempt to see if these age differences did alter
the overall savings rate. The life cycle information is based upon a study
of 1946 United States data and is presented in Table 7. Since the statistics
of Table 7 apply to spending units, it is necessary to convert the population
to these units. Headship rates for two years, 1890 and 1930, are available
in Population Changes and Building Cycles,[1] and are presented in Table 8.

---

[1]Burnham O. Campbell, Population Change and Building Cycles
(Urbana, University of Illinois, 1966), p. 186, Table 25.

Headship rates are defined as the proportion of any age group that are heads of spending units.

TABLE 7

INCOME AND SAVINGS LIFE CYCLE STATISTICS[a]

Age of head of spending unit	Income mean ratio[b]	Mean savings as a % of mean income
18-24	57	-3
25-34	95	6
35-44	118	12
45-64	116	13
65+	57	10

[a]Source: Janet A. Fisher, "Income, Spending, and Savings Patterns of Consumer Units in Different Age Groups," Output, Employment, and Productivity in the United States after 1800 (Studies in Income and Wealth, Vol. XV, Conference on Research in Income and Wealth; New York: National Bureau of Economic Research, 1952), p. 92, Table 10.

[b]The income mean ratio is defined as the percentage of total income received by spending units in a particular age group divided by the percentage of the total spending unit population in that age group times 100.

The 1890 rates of Table 8 are used for calculating 1870, 1880, 1890, 1900, and 1910 savings rates and the 1930 headship figures for calculating the 1920 savings rates. Since the headship rates start at age 15 and the savings data at age 18, I decided to apply the 18 - 24 savings rate to the 15 - 24 population. The earlier age of entry into the work force

TABLE 8

HEADSHIP RATES

Age	1890 (%)		1930 (%)
15-19	0. 6		0. 7
20-24	10. 7		11. 7
25-29	27. 3		
30-34	38. 5		32. 8
35-39	45. 1		
40-44	47. 9		44. 9
45-49	51. 6		
50-54	53. 4		50. 4
55-59	56. 0	(55-64)	53. 7
60+	51. 8	(65+)	53. 2

TABLE 9

SAVINGS RATES OF POPULATION GROUPS

Year	Total Population	Native white with native parents
1870	10. 32	
1880	10. 42	
1890	10. 42	10. 52
1900	10. 49	10. 55
1910	10. 53	10. 50
1920	10. 63	10. 49

during this period would probably justify this. However, since a very small portion of the population was the head of a spending unit during this age period, this adjustment makes very little difference in the final results.

The method of calculating the savings rates is indicated by the following formulation:

(Total savings for any age group) = (income per spending unit for age group) X (savings rate per spending unit for age group) X (number of spending units in age group), where income per spending unit for any given age group equals the income mean ratio for that age group.

The sum of the savings for all age groups divided by total income gives the savings rate. The results of the calculations are presented in Table 9.

The most meaningful comparison in Table 9 is between total population and the native born with native parents. The second column, in effect, presents the savings rate that would have existed in the absence of immigration, since it is based on the age structure of the native families. It is evident that the immigrants altered the savings of the entire economy very little. Therefore, if immigrants did influence capital formation through savings, it was not because of the difference in age structure of their population.

However, this conclusion rests upon the validity of the assumptions on which the calculations are made. The differences in age of the native and foreign born are an established fact, and fairly contemporary headship rates are used in converting these statistics to the number of spending units per population group. The most tenuous of the assumptions, therefore, is that savings rates for 1946 apply to the nineteenth century. In particular, changes in earning patterns and in family structure could have seriously altered savings habits between the latter part of the nineteenth century and the middle of the twentieth. In order to check the sensitivity of my calculations to changes in savings rates over time, I have recalculated a portion of Table 9, using alternative data. The date for which I have made these calculations is 1890, the earliest year for which I have age structure information for both the total population and different nativity groups within it.

First let us assume that the savings curve was much flatter in 1890 than in 1946. This can be explained by a much more extended family structure at the earlier date. The fact that each family was expected to provide for the financial security of its elder members could have reduced savings during the high income years, since each individual would have less incentive to save, knowing that provision had been made for his or her old age. With less education and an earlier age of entrance into the work force, dissavings might have been much less at the younger ages also. The hypothetical savings rates are presented below.

Age	Mean savings as a % of mean income
18-24	5
25-34	10
35-44	10
45-64	8
65+	5

In making the calculations using these savings rates I have assumed that the income mean ratio is the same as in Table 7. These alternative rates yield a savings rate of 8.80 per cent for the entire population and 8.76 per cent for the native white of native parents. Therefore, it cannot be argued that the more extended family structure of the nineteenth century would have altered my statistics so as to reveal a large scale influence of the foreign born on savings. In order to see if my results are sensitive to changes in the savings rates in the other direction, I have also made my calculations with a savings curve that starts lower, rises to a much higher level than the 1946 curve, and drops more sharply for the last group. In this case the savings rate for the total population with the presence of the foreign born would have been 14.61 per cent and for the native white-native parents 14.67. Although the immigrants would have lowered the savings rate in this case, again the difference between the two rates is negligible. The savings rates on which these calculations are based are presented below.

Age	Mean savings as a % of mean income
18-24	-5
25-34	10
34-44	15
45-64	20
65+	5

One last calculation was made to see if the application of the 1946 income mean ratios could have biased my results. I have assumed a much flatter earning curve, and have also assumed that the earlier age of entry raised incomes for the first age group. The alternative income mean ratios are presented below.

Age	Income mean ratio
18-24	70
25-34	100
35-44	110
45-64	105
65+	60

In this calculation of savings rates I have assumed that the age group savings rates were the same as presented in Table 7. With these alternative income mean ratios, the savings rate for the total population would have been 10.13 per cent and for the native white with native parents, 10.23 per cent.

It is evident from these examples that any plausible savings rates by age will not yield results markedly different from those reported in the first part of this section. The immigrants, while differing in age from the native born, could not have influenced overall savings much through this difference. Thus it has been shown that the age structure differences between the immigrants and native born were not major influences on growth, both in the area of labor force participation rates and savings.

Immigration and Internal Migration

All of the previous sections of this chapter have dealt with the economic impact of immigrants, but this impact has usually been discussed in terms of the aggregate economy. Although the influence of the immigrants has been shown to have been small in the total economy, this does not lessen the possibility that they could have seriously altered the economic position of certain individuals or groups in the country. Likewise, although the final equilibrium position might have been little different from what it would have been in the face of immigration, the movement to this equilibrium could have been changed by the presence of the foreign born. One way in which this could have happened was through the immigrants' effect on the necessity for internal migration in the nation. The United States was a rapidly changing economy during the period of heavy immigration, with her resources requiring considerable reallocation. The costs of labor reallocations are high, and the fact that there were numerous people entering the country each year could have lowered these costs for the native born. The immigrants had already borne most of the costs, both psychic and monetary, of migration upon arrival in this country. They could go to areas and industries where the demand for labor was the highest, thus eliminating the need for so many of the native born to move.

One of the largest movements of the nineteenth century and early twentieth century was the off-farm migration. The fact that most immigrants went into urban areas and only a small percentage entered agricultural occupations lessened the need for the native born to leave their farms. In order to measure this impact I have assumed that the immigrants did not alter the production functions of the nation, and that the increment they added to the demand for agricultural products increased the income of farmers in the same proportion as they increased non-agricultural incomes.[1] Thus the ratio of agricultural to non-agricultural income would have remained constant. If this ratio determined the relative number of people employed in agricultural and non-agricultural occupations, the ratio of persons in these two categories would have been

---

[1] This neglects the foreign trade sector of the United States. This was probably most important in agriculture. It could have been that immigrants did not increase the demand for certain agriculture products significantly in that these immigrants had been purchasers of these same U. S. products in their countries of origin. To the extent that this was true my results overstate the required movement out of agriculture; thus I overestimate the benefits from immigration.

the same in the absence of immigration as it was with the foreign born present.

These assumptions, although somewhat restrictive, allow one to calculate the off-farm movement that would have been required had immigration not taken place. For instance 47.4 per cent of the employed population worked in agriculture in 1870.[1] If this same percentage would have held without the foreign born present, considerable off-farm migration would have been necessary because 54.1 per cent of the native born labor force was in agriculture.[2] In order to achieve the same ratio of agricultural to non-agricultural workers as existed with the foreign born present, 657,000 native born would have had to migrate. Table 10 gives these same calculations for census years 1870 through 1920, excluding 1900, for which data is not available. Of course, column one cannot be summed to yield the total number of native born that would have had to move off farms. Rather the table does indicate that at any given date throughout this period approximately one tenth of the native born agricultural labor force would have had to move to maintain the same agricultural-non-agricultural work force ratio as existed with immigration. Although it is difficult to measure the impact this reduction in migration had on the economy, the evidence

[1]U. S. Department of Commerce, Bureau of the Census, Ninth Census of the United States, 1870, I, Population, 698-9.

[2]U. S. Department of Commerce, Bureau of the Census, Ninth Census of the United States, 1870, I, Population, 698-9.

TABLE 10

REQUIRED OFF-FARM MIGRATION IN THE ABSENCE OF IMMIGRATION, 1870-1920[a]

Census year	(1) Number of native born	(2) Percentage of native born agricultural work force
1870	657,000	12.0
1880	729,000	10.6
1890	725,000	9.4
1910	1,545,000	13.0
1920	1,114,000	11.0

[a]Calculated from: 1870: U. S. Department of Commerce, Bureau of the Census, Ninth Census of the United States, 1870, I, Population, 698-9. 1880: U. S. Department of Commerce, Bureau of the Census, Tenth Census of the United States, 1880, Compendium, pp. 1359-1360. 1890: U. S. Department of Commerce, Bureau of the Census, Eleventh Census of the United States, 1890, II, Population, cxvii. 1910 and 1920: U. S. Department of Commerce, Bureau of the Census, Fourteenth Census of the United States, 1920, IV.

shows that the immigrants aided in the United States' adjustment process to an industrial nation. Certainly considerable savings did result for individuals who did not have to bear the costs of moving to a different location and occupation within the country. These calculations have been carried out for only one, although perhaps the largest one, of the many migration processes that were taking place this period of history. The immigrants undoubtedly lessened the need for movement out of other geographical areas and occupations as well.

Economies of Scale

Several models employed in the thesis have assumed constant returns to scale. Although it is possible to relax this assumption in each of the models, it seems better to treat the question of non-constant returns in a more general way than the specific models allow.

It can be argued that the assumption of constant returns to scale is not valid for the growing nineteenth century economy, particularly with under-utilization of certain resources, the most oft-mentioned one being land. Although the possibility of decreasing returns to scale cannot be ruled out on theoretical grounds, it seems highly implausible that, for the economy as a whole, decreasing returns could have held. However, it does not seem so implausible to argue that increasing returns to scale were the rule rather than the exception during the period of major immigration. If increasing returns were existent, it is obvious that the immigrants affected total growth more than under constant returns, and that they also altered the per capita income of the native born population. I do not attempt to measure the extent of economies of scale from 1840 through 1920, but I do calculate the extent to which the immigrants affected the per capita income of the population if certain economies of scale held.

In attempting to measure sources of economic growth in a more recent period, Denison assumes that "in the 1929-57 period economies of scale increased the contribution of all other sources to economic growth by 10 per cent."[1] I have assumed that the same degree of increasing returns held for the period of immigration, 1840-1920. One might argue that this is an underestimate of the increasing returns for that period, but one should remember that this figure applies to the whole economy over an 80 year time span. Although there were undoubtedly certain industries that enjoyed increasing returns of greater than 10 per cent for certain portions of that time period, it seems unlikely that 10 per cent is an underestimate for all of the economy for the entire period.

In assessing the impact of immigration through economies of scale, one must make certain assumptions about what happened to the capital stock when immigration increased the labor force. Two extreme possibilities are discussed,[2] although it is probable the actual case lay somewhere between the two. The first possibility is that the growth of capital depended on the savings propensities of the population. Then the amount national income was increased depends on the amount of capital immigrants brought with them. If they brought no capital, income was

---

[1] Edward F. Denison, The Source of Economic Growth in the United States and the Alternatives Before Us (Supplementary Paper No. 13; Washington: Committee for Economic Development, 1962), p. 175.

[2] These possibilities are discussed ibid., p. 177.

increased by 1. 1 times labor's share of national income; i. e. , if labors' share was 0. 5 a 1 per cent increase in the labor force through immigration increased national income 0. 55 per cent. After the initial increase in income of 0. 55 per cent income increased at its original rate, assuming the immigrants have the same saving propensity as the native born. This case of course implies a permanent lowering of the capital-labor ratio.

On the other hand, if there existed an optimum capital-labor ratio determined by savings and investment conditions of the society, then following immigration this ratio was restored; a 1 per cent increase in the labor force implied a 1 per cent increase in the capital stock. The extreme of this case assumes that the adjustment took place immediately, that is, there was no lag between the increase of the labor force through immigration and the concomitant increase in the capital stock. I will argue that the most realistic case is for the capital-labor ratio to return to its original level, but that it did so only after a lag of several years.

Under the assumption of increasing returns an increase of the labor force through immigration causes fairly substantial increases in total income; however, the increases in per capita income are less than one might expect. Denison calculates the effect on per capita income of a 10 per cent increase in labor under the two alternative assumptions about the growth of capital.[1] The results are reported be-

low:

	Effect of increasing returns of 9 per cent on per capita income
Rate of capital accumulation unaffected	-1. 4%
Capital-labor ratio restored	+0. 5%

In assessing the impact of immigration through increasing returns

one has to determine how much of the population increase for the period

1840-1920 was because of immigration. In most of my previous discus-

sion I have assumed that the foreign born population, or at the most the

foreign born and their children, were the result of immigration. Since

most of the other analysis is concerned with differences between the

immigrant and non-immigrant population and since these differences be-

come much less important after a generation, this assumption seems

reasonable for those discussions. However, in discussing economies

of scale it is important to measure the total contribution of immigrants

to population growth, no matter through how many generations this was

extended. The obvious difficulty in terming all members of the popu-

lation that have foreign ancestors as "the result of immigration" is that

---

[1]Ibid., p. 177. Denison bases his calculations on a labor share
of 0.773, a capital share of 0.197, and a land share of 0.03. However,
he assumes land is fixed in supply so the increasing returns operate
only on labor and capital. In my calculations of the immigration period
I assume labor's share is 0. 50 and capital's is 0. 50. This implies land
is not fixed and is measured as capital.

one discovers that except for those of American Indian stock, all of the

population was here because of immigration of one period or another.

Since I am concerned with the immigration from 1840 through 1920 I have

chosen to approach the problem in another way. If there had been no immi-

gration from 1840 through 1920 what would have been the population in 1920?

That is, if the country would have had to depend on natural population growth

for the period, given the stock of 1840, what would the population increase

have been? Then one can term the difference between the actual population

growth and the growth that would have occurred just with natural increase

as the result of immigration.

There are some problems with this approach in that it is difficult

to determine what natural population increase would have been without im-

migration. Indeed some authors have argued that the native birth rate was

lowered so much by immigration that the total population was not altered at

all through the inflow from abroad. Although it is unlikely that there was

that much interdependence between immigration and the birth rate, it is

likely that they were not completely independent. However, it is not too

difficult to put a minimum figure on the contribution of natural growth of

population increase, thus obtaining a maximum for the contribution of im-

migration. Conrad and Irene Taeuber list the natural increase of the popu-

lation for each decade from 1810 through 1920.[1] I have calculated the

---

[1]Conrad Taeuber and Irene B. Taeuber, The Changing Population
of the United States (New York: John Wiley and Sons, Inc., 1958), Table
91, p. 294.

annual rate of natural increase for each of the decades for 1840 through 1920, and this information is presented in the following table.

TABLE 11

NATURAL POPULATION INCREASE, 1840-1920

Decade	Natural increase, annual percentage
1840-1850	2.46%
1850-1860	2.19%
1860-1870	1.84%
1870-1880	1.83%
1880-1890	1.41%
1890-1900	1.39%
1900-1910	1.20%
1910-1920	1.19%

It has been argued that the immigrants lowered the birth rate of the native population; therefore, one might suppose that in the absence of immigration the rate of increase would have been higher than that in the table. However, it should be noted that the rate of natural increase for each decade is based upon the population present at the beginning of that decade, therefore it includes the rate of increase of the immigrants present at the beginning of each decade. Since the foreign born had slightly larger families than the native born this could cause the rates of the table to overstate the rate of increase that would have existed in the absence of immigration. In order to ascertain the maximum effect of immigration upon population growth I have assumed that the annual rate of increase of the population in the absence of immigration would have been as follows:

1840-1860	2.00%
1860-1880	1.75%
1880-1900	1.25%
1900-1920	1.125%

If the above rates of natural increase were applied to the population of 1840 the population would have increased to 57.7 million in 1920. This implies that natural increase would have been responsible for 45.4 per cent of the increase of population from 1840 through 1920 and immigration 54.6 per cent. Since the rates of the above table probably understate the natural increase, it seems reasonable to assume that immigration contributed a maximum of 50 per cent to the population growth of the period.

One other important issue is the relationship between population increase and labor force increase. Denison's calculations, quoted on page 67, assume that the population increase and the labor force increase are equal; that is, a 10 per cent increase in the population implies a 10 per cent increase in the labor force. This would seem to be a safe assumption if all groups under consideration had similar labor force participation rates. However, since I am measuring the impact of the foreign born, a group with markedly different labor force participation rates from the

native born, one must adjust accordingly.

Population increased 522 per cent from 1840 through 1920. [1] If one

half of this was due to immigration, then immigrants and their offspring

increased the population 261 per cent. However, assuming labor force

participation rates of 1920 applied throughout the entire period for the

native and foreign born, [2] immigration was responsible for a 285 per cent

increase in the labor force. With increasing returns of 10 per cent, and

assuming that the increases of the labor force through immigration re-

sulted in an immediate and equal percentage increase in the capital stock,

immigration raised per capita income 21.9 per cent through economies of

scale. [3] One should note that a major contributor to the magnitude of the

effect was the difference in labor force participation rates of the native and

---

[1] United States Department of Commerce, Bureau of the Census, Historical Statistics of the United States, Colonial Times to 1957 (Washington, D. C.: Government Printing Office, 1960) Series A 1-3, p. 7.

[2] Labor force participation rates increased throughout the period under consideration. However, I assume the decrease in the average work week which was also occurring in this period exactly offset the labor force participation rate increase. In more recent periods the decrease in the work week has outweighed the participation rate increase. If this occurred in the 1840-1920 period my results overstate the effect of economies of scale.

[3] The magnitude of economies of scale is calculated by the equation: $Y^* = \alpha_1 L^* + \alpha_2 K^*$, where Y, L, and K represent income, labor, and capital respectively, the asterik indicates rate of change, and α_1 and α_2 represent the shares of labor and capital. Since economies of scale are

foreign born. If the immigrant population increase had resulted in an equal percentage increase in the labor force, per capita income would have been increased 13.6 per cent for the 1840-1920 period.

It would seem that the 21.9 per cent increase in per capita income is most likely an upper limit on the effect of immigration through economies of scale. Several things could have happened that would have reduced this effect. For instance, if economies of scale operated over a shorter period than the years 1840-1920, the effect would have been smaller. Also, if the inflow of labor through immigration permanently altered the capital-labor ratio, the effect on per capita income could even have been negative. Assuming capital and labor's share of output to be equal, if a 10 per cent increase of the labor force only implied an 8.18 per cent increase of capital, there would have been no effect on per capita income through economies of scale.[1] Therefore, if a 10 per cent increase of the labor force through immigration resulted in a less than 8 per cent increase in capital, per capita income would have been lowered; if it resulted in a greater than 8 per cent increase, it would have increased per capita income up to the maximum of 21.9 per cent for the 1840 through 1920 period.

---

assumed to be 10 per cent α_1 and α_2 are each set equal to 0.55. The change in per capita income is calculated with the equation $(Y + Y*)/(P + P*)$. Since I am dealing with large changes over long time spans, I have calculated all of my results on the basis of average annual rates of change in order that the above equations might more closely approximate the correct results.

[1] This again assumes economies of scale of ten per cent.

While it does seem reasonable to assume that the capital-labor ratio was not permanently altered by immigration, it also seems reasonable to assume that the growth of the capital stock did not immediately follow an increase of the labor supply. Of course, this assumes that the immigrants brought an amount of capital per worker less than the capital per worker present in the economy. I have assumed that immigration did not alter the long run capital-labor ratio, but that the adjustment to an increase in the labor force was not instantaneous. Rather, I have assumed that it took ten years for the capital stock to catch up after a given increase in the labor force through immigration, and that 10 per cent of this capital stock was made up in each of the ten years. Thus this implies that an immigrant worker brought capital with him equal to 10 per cent of the capital per laborer existing in the economy. In the second year the capital stock increased to 20 per cent of the increase in the labor force, the third year 30 per cent, until by the tenth year there was an increase in the total capital stock equal in percentage to the initial increase in the labor force.[1]

This can be illustrated by looking at one year in the immigration period, for instance, 1910. All immigration that occurred before 1901

---

[1]This can be represented by the equation: $K^* = 0.1L^*_t + 0.2L^*_{t-1} + 0.3L^*_{t-2} + \ldots \ldots 1.0L^*_{t-9}$, where K^* equals the percentage increase in capital for the years t-9 through t, and L^*_t equals the percentage increase in the labor force through immigration in year t. After K^* is calculated, the basic equation, $Y^* = \alpha_1 L^* + \alpha_2 K^*$ is used to calculate the effect of economies of scale.

resulted in a complete capital adjustment, i.e., a 50 per cent increase in the labor force by immigration prior to 1901 resulted in a 50 per cent increase in the capital stock by 1910. A 10 per cent increase in the labor force in 1910 due to immigration resulted in a 1 per cent increase in the capital stock. A 10 per cent increase in the labor force in 1909 resulted in a 2 per cent increase in the capital stock by 1910, and so on, with a 10 per cent increase in the labor force in 1902 resulting in a 9 per cent increase in the capital stock by 1910. This model assumes that the lag in capital occurred only when the labor force was increased directly by immigration. Increases that occurred through natural population growth (in this case natural growth means children of immigrants as well as children of the 1840 population) were foreseen, and the capital stock adjusted immediately upon their entrance into the population.

Assuming that capital and labor shared equally in output, with a ten year lag in capital accumulation, immigration caused a 20.5 per cent increase in per capita income in 1920 instead of the 21.9 per cent calculated under the assumption of instantaneous capital adjustment.

Summary and Conclusions

Although most of the economic impacts of the immigrants suggested by historians have been found to be fairly insignificant individually, this finding does not mean that the impact of all of the points considered is insignificant when considered in total. Therefore, it is necessary to use a summing process to calculate the total effect of the immigrants upon the economy. However, this process is difficult for two reasons. The first is that data limitations allow assessment of the effect of the immigrants to be made for only a limited number of dates during the immigration period. These dates do not coincide for all of the effects considered, therefore making a comparison for any one date difficult. The second is more important, the inherent conceptual problems that exist in speaking of the "effect" of any immigration impact. This effect must be felt by someone, and it is important to identify just who this someone is.

It would seem most natural to assess the effects in terms of the native born population present during the periods of immigration. However, several of the impacts discussed in the thesis are not relevant when the native born are selected as the "affected group." For instance, the section dealing with Immigration and Per Capita Income (page 37), discusses the effect of the higher labor force participation rates and lower labor force quality of the foreign born on the per capita income of the entire population. However, in the absence of externalities the labor force participation rates and quality of the immigrants would not affect the income position of the native born. Secondly, in the section entitled Immigration and Human Capital, I discuss the advantage gained by having a portion of the population educated outside of the United States, i.e., the immigrants. Again, however, if the population were just the native born of that date, it would be meaningless to talk of a savings of education costs on a population group that did not exist, the immigrants. Also, it is difficult to assess what

would have happened to the total growth rate in the absence of immigration
since most of the variables of Table 1, page 31, would have been significantly altered by such an absence.

These effects are of importance, and it is therefore necessary to
define a population group under which their impact can be assessed. A
hypothetical group can be suggested under which one can consider all but
two of the effects discussed previously in this chapter. One can ask the
counterfactual question; in the absence of immigration what would have
been the total and per capita income of the population at any given date if
the same number of residents would have existed as existed with immigration? Thus this counterfactual question assumes that the same amount
of population growth took place, but that it was all by natural means, rath
than a portion of it being through immigration. This hypothetical populati
group I term "Population I."

The two effects that do not lend themselves to this population grou
are (1) the first considered in the thesis, the effect on the population already present, and (2) the effect of economies of scale. However, there
is an effect from economies of scale on the hypothetical group suggested
above in that this group, although based upon the same population growth
as existed with immigration, does allow for labor force participation diffe
ences, and it is through these differences that much of the impact of
economies of scale is felt. Nevertheless, in order to fully assess the im
pact of economies of scale I offer a total effect for a second population

group, namely the native born population in the absence of immigration. Note that this group does not assume replacement of the foreign born by native born but measures the effect of the absence of immigration upon the native born population actually present during immigration. Hereafter it will be referred to as "Population II."

I have chosen to carry out the summing process for two dates in the immigration period, 1880 and 1910. Not all of the impacts discussed are calculated for both of these dates; therefore, some extrapolation is necessary. More of the calculations are carried out for 1880 than for any other date; consequently, it seemed an obvious one to choose. It is also about the earliest in the immigration period for which one can make any reasonably accurate calculation. It also seems desirable to measure the total impact towards the end of the immigration period; therefore, 1910 is chosen. It is superior to 1920 in that immigration from 1915 through 1920 was markedly affected by several factors, particularly World War I and the beginning of the quota restrictions. The annual rate of growth of the foreign born population was only 0.3 per cent from 1910 to 1920, whereas it had exceeded 1 per cent for every decade prior to that.

Table 12 presents the summary statistics for the two years, 1880 and 1910, and for the two population groups. The arguments for each of the effects are presented below. I do not include the first effect discussed in the chapter, the impact of immigration upon the population already present. There are two reasons for not doing so. First, for any plausible

TABLE 12

THE TOTAL EFFECT OF THE ABSENCE OF IMMIGRATION
ON PER CAPITA INCOME[a]

	1880		1910	
Effect (1)	Population Group I (2)	Population Group II (3)	Population Group I (4)	Population Group II (5)
Amounts (millions of dollars)				
1. Immigration and growth	-19.2	-16.7	+386.2	+329.4
2. Human capital	-26.1		-117.4	
3. Funds and remittances	+ 4.0	+ 4.0	+204.0	+204.0
4. Age structure and savings rates			+ 16.0	+ 13.6
5. Internal migration	-129.4	-103.5	-395.9	-321.4
6. Total of lines 1-5	-160.7	-115.9	+ 92.9	+225.6
Percentages				
7. Line 6 as a % of national income	- 1.96	- 1.63	+ 0.32	+ 0.9
8. Immigration and per capita income	- 2.56		- 1.00	
9. Economies of scale	- 3.01	-10.75	- 3.29	- 14.4

TABLE 12--Continued

	(1)	(2)	(3)	(4)	(5)
10.	Total percent-age change in per capita income	-7.53	-12.38	- 3.97	-13.57

[a]Since I am measuring the impact of the absence of immigration the positive sign (+) indicates an increase in income and a negative sign (-) indicates a decrease in income with such an absence.

values the effect is insignificant; second, it is essentially a short-run effect based upon alterations of the capital-labor ratio. In the following discussion I am concerned with the total effect of immigration for the two long-run periods, 1840-1880 and 1840-1910.

Immigration and Growth

The difference in the growth rate is assessed by assuming that P_f^* (see Table 2, page 32) would have continued but as P_n^*. That is, the same population growth would have existed, but as native growth. Also assume that K_f^* would have been the same, but in the form of K_n^*. Assume that the change in the native born labor force participation rate, Y_n^*, listed in Table 2, held for the entire population. Assume also $\lambda = 1$ and $\lambda * = 0$. Under these assumptions the growth rate from 1870-1880 would have been 3.88 per cent annually instead of 3.90; for 1880-1890, 3.47 per cent instead of 3.44; for 1890-1900, 2.49 instead of 2.55; and for 1900-1920,

3.09 instead of 2.91. I assume that the effect before 1870 was neutral

since the immigrants raised the growth rate in two of four decades and

lowered it in the other two. When these rates are converted to decade

rates and multiplied times GNP at the beginning of each of the decades

under consideration, one obtains values of Table 12, line 1, columns 2 and

4. It should be noted that the signs of the values of Table 12 denote the im

pact on income in the absence of immigration. Thus a negative sign indi-

cates that the absence of immigration from 1840 would have lowered

national income by the stated amount; a positive sign indicates national

income would have been increased by that amount. The fact that the native

and foreign born had different growth rates of labor force participation

rates and labor force quality would have resulted in national income 19.2

million lower for the period 1840-1880 and would have caused national in-

come to be 386.2 million higher for the period 1840-1910 in the absence

of immigration.

If there would have been no immigration and no replacement of the

foreign born by the native born, total growth would have been lowered, but

most of this lowering would not have affected the native born. It is not

clear that the differences in the native and foreign born population which

did affect the growth rate as indicated above directly affected the native

born that would have been present without immigration. However, in

order to estimate this effect if it were present, assume that the impact was proportional to the representation of the native born present in 1880 and 1910 in the population. Therefore the estimates for line 1, columns 3 and 5 are arrived at by multiplying the estimates of columns 2 and 4 by the percentage of the native born represented in the population. This assumption is not crucial to my results.

Human Capital

I calculate that the immigrants saved 24.093 million in education costs in the United States in 1880. In other words, it would have cost 24 million more to educate the population had it all been native born. If one assumes that physical capital formation would have been lowered by this amount, using Gallman's estimate of gross capital formation for 1880,[1] capital formation would have been 1.45 per cent lower in the absence of immigration. However, one must assess the effect of this lower capital formation over a period prior to 1880, since the capital stock of 1880 was a result of past accumulation. 1840 is generally regarded as the year that marks the beginning of the major movement of people to the United States. Therefore, I have assumed that physical capital formation from 1840 through 1880 would have been 1.45 percent lower if the United States had had to educate all of her citizens herself, i.e., in the absence of immigration. Gross capital formation during this period was

[1]Gallman, "Gross National Product in the United States, 1834-1908," Vol. XXX, p. 34.

approximately 30 billion dollars.[1] If capital formation would have been lowered 1.45 per cent throughout the period by the absence of immigration, the capital stock in 1880 would have been 435 million less than actually existed. If this capital stock yielded a six per cent return, income would have been decreased by 26.1 million.

It should be noted that this estimate contains an upward bias in that no allowance is made for depreciation.

This approach assumes that a certain portion of national income is allocated to capital formation, human and physical, and a savings in human capital costs is used for physical capital formation. Alternatively, if one wished to regard the savings on education in 1880 as simply as increase in income, no cumulative effect is present, and incomes would have been 24 million lower with no immigration but with a population of equal size.

Gross capital formation for the period 1840-1910 was approximately 135 billion.[2] If, with the same size population but with all education carried out in this country, capital formation would have been 1.45 per cent less, the capital stock would have been reduced by 1,957.5 million. Assuming a six per cent return, income would have been lowered by 117.4 million. This estimate is undoubtedly biased upwards since it assumes a reduction in capital formation, 1.45 per cent, equal

---

[1] Ibid.

[2] Ibid.

to that calculated for 1880. However, this calculation is based upon the immigrants who entered after 1880 who would have been of school age in 1880. The major immigration ended shortly after 1910, so there would not have been as great a saving on education costs for that date.

As noted before, only if one is discussing the hypothetical population group in which the foreign born are replaced by native born, can one argue that the country gained from an inflow of human capital. If there were no inflow, no gain would result; therefore, columns 3 and 5 of Table 12 note no human capital effect.

Funds and Remittances

There was an estimated outflow of 4 million dollars in 1880 and 204 million in 1910 because of an excess of remittances over funds brought. Therefore, the population would have been richer by these amounts if it had been all native born. It is assumed that income would have been increased by these amounts in the absence of immigration.

Age Structure and Savings Rates

Table 9, page 55, indicates that the savings rate would have been 0.10 of a per cent higher to 0.14 of a per cent lower in the absence of immigration. However, no estimate exists for dates prior to 1890. Since half of the effects are positive and half negative and are small in either case, assume that prior to 1890 the savings rate effect was neutral. Assume for the period 1890-1910 that the savings rate calculated for the beginning of the decade held throughout the decade. Then savings would have been 1 per cent higher in the period 1890-1900 and

0.6 per cent higher for the period 1900-1910 in the absence of immi-

gration. Personal savings estimates are not available for the nine-

teenth century, but the national wealth increased 17.7 billion from 1890

through 1899.[1] Assume 25 per cent of this was due to corporate and

government savings and the rest a result of personal savings. Personal

savings from 1900 through 1909 were 22.29 billion.[2] Therefore, if in

the absence of immigration the savings rate would have increased 1 per

cent and 0.6 per cent for the two periods, gross capital formation would

have been 267 million greater in 1910. If capital yielded a 6 per cent

return, income would have been 16 million greater.

Assume the effect would have been proportionate if just the native

born population were present. Therefore, since the native born were

85.3 per cent of the total population in 1910, the effect on the native

born would have been an increase in income of 13.6 million in the

absence of immigration.

Internal Migration

Table 10, page 63, lists 729,000 as the required off-farm

migration in the absence of immigration. However, this is the off-farm

migration that would have been required for the native born population

---

[1] Historical Statistics of the United States, Colonial Times to 1957, Series F-198, p. 151.

[2] Ibid. Series F-316, p. 156.

to maintain the same agricultural-non-agricultural occupation ratio. In order to put this figure in the context of the hypothetical population group in which the same size of the population is maintained, certain assumptions must be made. In 1880, 49.3 per cent of the native born were in agriculture. Assuming that the agriculture-non-agriculture labor force ratio that existed in 1880 would have represented equilibrium in the absence of immigration, 44.1 per cent of the population would have had to have been in agriculture. There were 3,495,000 foreign born in the work force. Under the assumptions of the hypothetical population group, these would have been replaced by native born. Assume these native born distributed themselves in the work force in the same proportion as the other native born, that is, those who actually existed. Then, in order to achieve the same agricultural-non-agricultural ratio as actually existed with immigration, 911,000 of the native born would have had to transfer from agricultural to non-agricultural occupations. This is compared to the 729,000 transfer required when one considers just the native born population.

Assume costs of transfer of $100 **per** worker and assume two months of income are foregone in the migration process. Easterlin estimates agriculture income per worker in 1880 as $252.[1] Therefore,

---

[1] Richard A. Easterlin, "Interregional Differences in Per Capita Income, Population, and Total Income, 1840-1950," Trends in the American Economy in the Nineteenth Century (Studies in Income and Wealth, Vol. XXIV, Conference on Research in Income and Wealth, A Report of the National Bureau of Economic Research; Princeton: Princeton University Press, 1960).

total migration costs would have been 129.4 million.

Under the same assumptions the required off-farm migration in 1910 would have been 1,903,000. The average annual earnings of farm labor in 1910 is estimated at $336.[1] In order not to impute a downward bias assume the yearly income of persons in agriculture to be $350. Assume $150 moving costs and 2 months foregone income. Then the total cost of the required migration in the absence of immigration would be 395.9 million.

If one considers the effect of the required migration on the native born present at any one point in time, then the figures of Table 10 apply. Under the same assumptions about moving costs and foregone earnings, the absence of immigration would have cost the native born 103.5 million in 1880 and 321.4 million in 1910.

Immigration and Per Capita Income

My estimates indicate that per capita income of the total population was from 1.1 to 3.8 per cent greater because of the presence of the immigrants.[2] However, these estimates exist for the years 1890 through 1920. In order to compare this effect with the other effects in 1880, some assumptions must be made. Table 4, page 41, lists the effect of the foreign born on per capita income before the labor force

---

[1] Historical Statistics of the United States, Colonial Times to 1957, Series D-613, p. 91.

[2] Table 5, p. 43 .

participation rates of the native born are adjusted to remove the child-ren of the foreign born, and the table also has this information for 1880. The estimates of Table 5 are from 18 to 43 per cent of the estimates of Table 4, with the average being 32.5 per cent. Therefore assume that for 1880 the estimate of Table 5 would be 32.5 per cent of the estimate of Table 4. This would mean that in 1880 per capita income was 2.63 per cent higher because of the immigrants, or using the population that actually existed as the base, income would have been 2.56 per cent lower without the immigrants. The estimate for 1910 is 1.1 per cent, or again converting using the actual population as the base, income would have been 1 per cent lower in the absence of immigration.

As noted previously, if one is discussing the effect of immigration upon the native born present at any given date, per capita income would not be altered in the sense that is discussed above. The higher per capita income is because of the higher labor force participation rates and the lower labor force quality of the foreign born, and the income position of the native born was not altered by these differences. Thus only in the context of the hypothetical population group of the same size as existed with immigration can this effect be present.

Economies of Scale

It might appear that economies of scale would not be operative under the hypothetical population group since it assumes equal popu-lation size both with and without immigration; however, this is not true.

One of the major reasons for proposing this counterfactual case is to assess the effects of differences between the native and foreign born. One of the major differences between the two groups was in labor force participation rates. Therefore, even if the population were of the same size with and without immigration, the fact that the presence of the immigrants meant a larger labor force would have had an impact if economies of scale were present.

Assume that if there had been no immigration and equal population growth occurred through natural means, the labor force in 1880 would have been determined by the 1880 labor force participation rate of the native born. In that case economies of scale of 10 per cent would have raised per capita income 11.2 per cent. However, with the immigration that actually existed, the labor force increase was greater, although population increase was the same. Then, with instantaneous capital adjustment, economies of scale over the period 1840-1880 raised per capita income 14.3 per cent. Thus the effect of immigration through economies of scale is the difference between these two effects, namely 3.1 per cent.

Likewise, using 1910 labor force participation rates, the difference between the increase in per capita income with the immigrants present and with them absent but with equal population growth is 3.4 per cent. Since I am discussing the effect on per capita income of the immigrants' absence, and since these percentages measure the increase in per capita income due to the immigrants' presence, conversion to a different base is necessary. When the percentages are expressed as the decrease in per capita income that would have occurred in the absence of immigration, they become 3.01 and 3.29 respectively.

If economies of scale were operative over the entire period to the degree of 10 per cent, and if no immigration had occurred and no replacement of the immigrant population is assumed, one gets fairly major effects on per capita income. For the period 1840-1880 per capita income would be reduced 10.75 per cent in the absence of immigration and for the period 1840-1910 the reduction would be 14.49 per cent. These figures assume the capital-labor ratio was restored after immigration but with a lag of ten years.

Summary

The effects of Table 12 which are expressed in dollar amounts (lines 1 through 5) can be totaled (line 6) and expressed as a percentage of national income (line 7).[1] Since the percentages of lines 8 and 9 refer to changes in per capita income of a population of the same size as is being considered in line 7, these percentages are then additive and when summed yield a total percentage effect on per capita income (line 10).

---

[1] I have used national income estimates of 8.16 billion and 28.7 billion for 1880 and 1910 respectively. For the calculations for population Group II I have assumed that national income would have been 87 per cent and 85 per cent of the actual estimates since these percentages represent the proportion of the native born in the total population for these dates.

These percentages express the decrease in per capita income that would have occurred in the absence of immigration for the two population groups on which I chose to measure the impact. It should be noted that although there are positive effects, i. e., in some cases the absence of immigration would have raised per capita income, that the net effect for each of the years and the two population groups is negative; that is, the absence of immigration would have lowered per capita income from 3. 97 per cent to 13. 57 per cent.

It is necessary to note that the magnitude of the effects is sharply influenced by what assumptions one makes about economies of scale. If the entire immigration period were not characterized by increasing returns to the extent I postulate, then the reduction in per capita income would have been much less. Of course, if economies of scale were greater than 10 per cent for the period, my estimates understate the impact of immigration.

It is difficult to label the percentages of Table 12 as significant or insignificant since it is not clear what such terms mean quantitatively. However, it does seem that many of the impacts that were labeled by the historians as being important are not so very crucial when subjected to measurement. It is also interesting to note that if the immigrants did have a major impact, it was through economies of scale, an issue usually not discussed by immigration writers.

It is difficult to argue that a 13 per cent decrease in income in

1910 would not have been important to a resident of the country at that date. However, it is important to remember that this effect is the sum of the effects of the absence of immigration for 70 years. During that period real GNP per head increased from approximately $200 to approximately $650.[1] This is a 225 per cent increase, and immigrants were responsible for between 2 and 6 per cent of it. The increase in real GNP per head for 1840-1880 was approximately 100 per cent,[2] and, therefore, immigration was responsible for approximately 7-12 per cent of this increase.

When historians speak of immigration as being crucial to the process of economic growth, it is hard to cast such statements in quantitative terms. However, much of the literature leads one to believe that the immigrants were responsible for much more than 2-12 per cent of the growth of per capita income during the period.

Undoubtedly, there are many ways in which the immigrants could have affected the United States which have not been tested. They could have been carriers of technological information; they might have brought a new spirit of entrepreneurship to this country. Of course, the whole area of the non-economic impact of the immigrants is not discussed in this paper. The foreign born were obviously important to the

---

[1]Raymond Goldsmith, Testimony before the U. S. Congress Joint Economic Committee, printed in Employment, Growth, and the Price Level, 86th Congress, 1st Session, Part II, 1959 (Washington: Government Printing Office, 1959), Chart IV, p. 238.

[2]Ibid.

the cultural, political, and social life of the nation. Nevertheless, almost all of the hypotheses presented in the historical literature that are concerned with the immigrants effect on the economy have been discussed and tested in this chapter and found lacking. Every previous writer has pictured immigration as a major force in changing the course of economic development in this country. It seems much more fitting to speak of the nineteenth and early twentieth century influx into the United States as simply an efficient means in increasing the population and the labor force. This meant an alteration of per capita and national income if economies of scale existed. Otherwise, immigration had only a small effect on per capita income and the effect on national income was little different from what it would have been with a higher birth rate on the part of the native born population.

CHAPTER III

WAGE DATA AND THE RELATIVE SKILLS OF
THE NATIVE AND FOREIGN BORN

In the chapter preceding this one, one of the more important statistics derived and used was λ , a measure of the relative labor force quality of the foreign born. My results indicated that the labor force quality of the native and foreign born were very close, with the foreign born labor force ranking slightly below the native born and ranging from a high of . 99 in 1880 to a low of . 93 in 1920. My results disagree quite sharply with the evaluation of immigrant workers expressed in the literature. Although much of the concern over low foreign labor force quality centers around the recent immigrants, if my index is correct, it means that either the entering workers were not very different from the native born or that they advanced very rapidly. The variance of my conclusions and those of the historians demand further evidence on this question. This chapter discusses additional information that is useful in checking on the validity of my conclusions.

Naturally wages and earnings of native and foreign born are good indices of relative labor force quality but no complete wage series is available encompassing a significant portion of the population during most

93

of the period and also differentiating between foreign born and native

workers. Therefore, to measure quality differences I used the relative

skills of the two nativities, weighted by relative wage rates for these

skills. However, wage data which makes adequate differentiation among

workers is available for certain industries for a few selected dates during

the period of immigration. These are not sufficient to construct an over-

all index of relative labor force quality, but they are informative and

serve as checks on my other index.

The first data of interest is contained in the Sixth Annual Report

of the Commissioner of Labor for 1890 and is entitled Cost of Production

Iron, Steel, Coal, etc. [1] This report is based on 618 establishments and

the earnings data of interest is assembled from budget studies of 2,490

families. The Report does not state how many of the 618 establishments

are represented in the budget study, but a geographical and industry list-

ing of the budgets is available and is reproduced in Table 13. This table

shows that the budgets represent a fairly wide sample, across six indus-

tries and ten states. No claim is made for complete randomness, but

data based upon these budgets is seemingly representative of a major

segment of nineteenth century American industry. The 2,490 families

are classified by nativity by the place of birth of the head of the family,

and of these 2,490, 1,294 are native born and 1,196 are foreign born.

---

[1] United States Commissioner of Labor, Sixth Annual Report of the
Commissioner of Labor, 1890, Cost of Production: Iron, Steel, Coal,
Etc. (Washington: Government Printing Office, 1891).

Since only 15 per cent of the population in 1890 was foreign born, the
sample is biased towards the immigrant population. The English, Irish,
German, and Welsh are most heavily represented in the study, and they
make up 84 per cent of the total foreign born. Income information is
given in the form of yearly earnings per family from the husband and
from all sources. The income per family from the husband is $520.43
for the native born and $549.81 for the foreign born. The total family in-
come for the foreign born is also greater than that of the native born,
$663.81 compared to $583.68. In order to compare the results of this
study with my previous measure, λ , I have computed incomes for the

TABLE 13

NUMBER OF BUDGETS TABULATED, IRON, STEEL, AND COAL[a]

State	Pig Iron	Bar Iron	Steel	Bituminous Coal	Coke	Iron Ore	Total
Alabama	143	39	2	60	30		274
Georgia	25						25
Illinois	40	68	38				146
Indiana				36			36
New York	56	41	62			38	197
Ohio	98	140	8	103		29	378
Pennsylvania	313	277	48	301	187	73	1199
Tennessee	51	17			15	9	92
Virginia	27	35		8		16	78
West Virginia	9	6	25		17		65

[a]U. S. Commissioner of Labor, Sixth Annual Report, p. 605.

major national groups and the total foreign born as a percentage of native

born income. This, along with information on family size, is presented

in Table 14.

These results, of course, are even stronger indicators than my

previous index that the foreign born were not inferior laborers relative

to the native born. Another interesting fact is that although the immi-

grant husbands earned more than the native husbands, the foreign born

families raised their total income even further above that of the native

born. This of course was done by taking in boarders and children and

wives working. My previous index reported a relative labor force quality

of .95 for 1890, and since these figures indicate a foreign born quality

even higher than this, they certainly do not indicate an upward bias in

the index. It should also be remembered that this data is based upon a

small sample of the population and just covers one portion of a major in-

dustrial group, whereas the previous index is based upon the entire

population in all occupational groups.

Further available information throws even more doubt upon the

historical conclusion that the immigrants were a much exploited, eco-

nomically deprived class. Of the 1194 foreign born families in this study,

236, or 25 per cent, owned their own homes, while only 18 per cent of

the native born owned theirs.[1]

---

[1] U. S. Commissioner of Labor, Sixth Annual Report, p. 1375,
Table 24, G.

TABLE 14

RELATIVE INCOMES OF NATIVE AND FOREIGN BORN,
THE IRON, COAL, AND STEEL INDUSTRIES, 1890[a]

Nativity of Husband	Number of Families	Family Size	Income as a % of Native Born Income	
			Husband	Total Family Income
United States	1, 294	4. 8	100	100
English	238	5. 1	103	109
German	276	5. 0	109	109
Irish	385	5. 5	106	119
Welsh	111	5. 4	118	132
Total Foreign Born	1, 196	5. 2	106	114

[a]U. S. Commissioner of Labor, Sixth Annual Report, p. 1374,
Table 24, F.

The tables in the report which summarize these budget studies
list the number of families at the end of the year having a surplus, those
having a deficit, and the average surplus and deficit. From this data one
can calculate the percentage of income saved, although this does not meet
the correct definition of savings. Part of the expenditures during the
year were possibly forms of savings, i.e., bonds, and this is not re-
corded in the year's end surplus. Nevertheless, a comparison can be
made between the native and foreign born for this particular definition of
savings, where savings is just considered as the net balance held at the

end of the year. When one carries out the calculations for this, one dis-

covers that savings rates were very similar for the native and foreign

born, 10.5 per cent for the native and 10.8 per cent for the foreign.

The second set of wage data that is available is contained in the

next Annual Report of the Commissioner of Labor, the Seventh, for

1891.[1] It deals with three industries, glass and cotton and woolen tex-

tiles and represents budget studies from 23 states. In this case glass

manufacturing is reported separately from the textile manufacturing.

Of 1,276 families in the sample from the glass industry, 440 of them are

foreign when classified by nativity of the head of the family. The cotton

and woolen sample consists of 3,043 families, 1,482 of them foreign.

The summary statistics for the glass industry are presented in Table 15,

with the same measure used as previously, income as a percentage of

native born income. Again the foreign born have a higher income than

the native born, although the difference is not so great as in the Sixth

Annual Report. Here 29 per cent of the foreign born own their homes,

while 25 per cent of the native born own theirs. Using the same concept

of savings as previously, the native have a savings rate of 10.1 per cent,

and the foreign born 11.4 per cent.

The summary statistics for the cotton and woolen industries are

---

[1]U. S. Commissioner of Labor, Seventh Annual Report of the
Commissioner of Labor, 1891, Cost of Production: The Textiles and
Glass, II, Part III, The Cost of Living (Washington: Government
Printing Office, 1891).

TABLE 15

RELATIVE INCOMES OF THE NATIVE AND FOREIGN BORN,
THE GLASS INDUSTRY, 1891[a]

Nativity of Husband	Number of Families	Family Size	Income as a % of Native Born Income	
			Husband	Total Family Income
United States	836	4.8	100	100
English	59	4.9	105	102
French	20	5.1	115	114
German	231	4.9	98	97
Irish	94	5.2	97	105
Total Foreign Born	440	5.0	102	103

[a]U. S. Commissioner of Labor, Seventh Annual Report, p. 1733, Table XXVIII, G.

presented in Table 16. Again the major national groups are listed, along with the figures for the total foreign born. Perhaps the most interesting statistics in this table is the sharp difference between the income of the husband and that of the total family for the foreign born. Although the foreign born husband's earnings are the same as those of the native husband, the total family income is significantly higher than that of the native born. This fact contrasts with the glass industry, where both immigrant husbands and immigrant families have incomes comparable to those of the native born. Part of the explanation for this may lie in the fact that average incomes are much lower in the textile industries than in glass. The average husband's income is $430.19 in the textile industries, but it is

$771.81 in glass. This lower income may have given the foreign family

added impetus to increase their income, but it is not clear why the native

family did not also feel this impetus. The savings rates are not very

different for the textile industries, 8.5 per cent for the native born and

7.8 per cent for the foreign born.

TABLE 16

RELATIVE INCOMES OF NATIVE AND FOREIGN BORN,
THE COTTON AND WOOLEN INDUSTRIES, 1891[a]

Nativity of Husband	Number of Families	Family Size	Income as a % Native Born Income	
			Husband	Total Family Income
United States	1561	5.2	100	100
Canadian	98	6.2	89	117
English	353	5.1	113	122
French Canadian	226	6.8	86	127
German	160	5.1	98	105
Irish	468	6.1	94	129
Scotch	81	5.3	123	137
Total Foreign Born	1482	5.8	100	124

[a]U. S. Commissioner of Labor, Seventh Annual Report, p. 1761,
Table XXX, F.

The differences in specific national groups in Tables 14, 15, and

16 show no clear pattern. The oft-stated hypothesis about the lower

productiveness of the Irish is borne out in a mild way, but it should also be noted that they, while lagging in husband's income, always raise the total family income above that of the total foreign born.

One of the most significant bodies of data which throws light upon the question of native-foreign differences is the Eighteenth Annual Report of the Commissioner of Labor, published in 1903.[1] For the most part the data collected in this report deals with the calendar year 1901, covering 25,440 families, of which 10,279 are foreign, with nativity again assigned by the birthplace of the head of the family. The sample covers 33 states and "the number of family schedules to be secured in each of the several selected was roughly apportioned according to the number of persons employed in the manufacturing industries of the States. . . ."[2] The sample covers only wage workers and salaried people with salaries below $1,200. This undoubtedly biases the sample somewhat, but since the average income of husbands is about one-half of that, it is doubtful that this imparts a substantial bias to the figures. In this case average income of husbands is $637.22 for the native born and $597.19 for the foreign born. Total family income is $742.00 for the native born, and $760.57 for the foreign born.[3] Since the sample is much larger than previous ones, it is

[1]U.S. Commissioner of Labor, Eighteenth Annual Report of the Commissioner of Labor, 1903 (Washington: Government Printing Office, 1904).

[2]Ibid., p. 15.

[3]Ibid., Table III, J.

TABLE 17

RELATIVE INCOMES OF NATIVE AND FOREIGN BORN,
EIGHTEENTH ANNUAL REPORT, 1903[a]

Nativity of Husband	Number of Families	Family Size	Income as a % of Native Born Income	
			Husband	Total Family Income
United States	15,161	4.67	100	100
Austria-Hungary	283	5.04	85	91
Canada	1,012	5.16	97	107
Denmark	103	5.05	105	102
England	930	4.90	106	111
France	86	4.95	94	101
Germany	2,883	5.24	92	100
Ireland	2,983	5.26	90	104
Italy	256	5.02	80	82
Netherlands	104	5.72	81	91
Norway	154	5.32	103	103
Russia	443	5.70	84	89
Scotland	251	5.08	107	116
Sweden	502	4.78	102	103
Switzerland	57	4.88	100	104
Wales	119	5.26	97	108
Other Foreign Born	113	4.84	95	96
Total Foreign Born	10,279	5.18	94	103

[a]U. S. Commissioner of Labor, Eighteenth Annual Report, Table III, J.

possible to report the income position of more national groups. A summary of the relative income positions is presented in Table 17.

The rather large sample of Table 17 which covers numerous industries in manufacturing also lends support to the conclusions drawn from the index of Chapter II. The figure arrived at there for 1900 is 97 compared to the 94 of this study, which is relatively close considering the different methods of constructing the indices. Although the overall foreign born population seems to have been quite comparable to the native population, there were significant differences between the native born and certain immigrant groups as is evident from Table 17. The four lowest ranking income of husband are Italy, the Netherlands, Russia, and Austria-Hungary. Since three of these four are among those countries classified as part of the "new immigration" this might lend support to the view that this new immigration was markedly different than the old and that it was made up of less-skilled, less productive workers. However, an alternative explanation exists; if immigrants entered the country low on the economic ladder and if they then advanced fairly rapidly, the low incomes of these groups would be explained by the much larger proportion of the recent immigrants in their midst, rather than by actual national differences. Further testing would be required to evaluate these two alternative hypotheses.

Other figures available from this report include percentage of home owners, 15 per cent for the native born and 24 per cent for the foreign born, and savings rates, 6.8 per cent for the native born and 6.6 per cent for the foreign born.[1] Again savings is computed on the basis of income unexpended at the end of the year. Another measure that indicates the closeness of the economic position of the two groups is the percentage of income spent on food: 46 per cent for the native born and 44 per cent for the foreign born.

The three reports cited in this chapter and summarized in Tables 14, 15, 16, and 17 lend strong support to the proposition that the economic position and the productivity of the native and foreign born were very close. Although there are certain national groups that had income positions lower than the native born, these do not seem to have been a significant portion of the immigrant population. One could argue however, that the relative earnings of the previous tables do not accurately reflect the relative productivities of the native and foreign born because of differences between the two populations. The major difference that comes to mind is age; it could be that the foreign born were less productive over their entire lifetime than the native born, but because more of them were in the high income earning age groups, a cross-section based on any one point in time would indicate very similar earnings for the two groups. None of the wage data reported in previous tables allows any comparison of earnings by age so it is not possible to directly test this possibility. However, by looking

[1] U. S. Commissioner of Labor, Eighteenth Annual Report, p. 67.

at the age structure of the nativity groups from the various censuses and applying modern life cycle earnings data one can gain some insight into the question.

I have used the same life cycle earnings statistics as I used previously in calculating the effect of age structure on savings rates.[1] Since the income mean ratios are for household units I have converted the nativity groups with which I am concerned to spending units by the same headship rates as used previously.[2] Using this data and data on the age structure of the various nativity groups I have calculated the incomes of these nativity groups assuming age differences is the only factor influencing income. I have made a comparison between the nativity groups for the four census years for which I have complete data, 1890, 1900, 1910, and 1920; and the results are reported below.

In 1890 foreign born earnings were 2.0 per cent higher than native white of native parent earnings and 1.8 per cent higher than the total population's earnings because of differences in age structure.

In 1900 foreign born earnings were 0.5 per cent greater than earnings of native white of native parents and 0.8 per cent higher than those of the total population because of differences in age structures.

In 1910 foreign born earnings were 0.5 per cent higher than earnings of the native white of native parents and 1.5 per cent lower than

---

[1]Table 7, p. 54.

[2]Table 8, p. 55.

earnings of the total population because of differences in age structure.

Therefore it seems that age structure differences were not im-

portant influences in the relative earnings of the native and foreign born

populations. One other possible influence on earnings that has not been

considered is discrimination against the foreign born. Several historians

have argued that the immigrants suffered considerable discrimination and

low earnings as a consequence of it. None of my data allows one to dis-

tinguish between wage differences which were the result of quality differ-

ences and those which were caused by discrimination. However, in view

of the similarity of earnings of the native and foreign born either dis-

crimination was not a strong force or immigrant labor force quality was

enough higher than the native born to overcome the discrimination. The

former hypothesis appears to be the most plausible.

In none of the studies cited to date are there indications of the

exploitation of the immigrants or the complete lack of skills and conse-

quent low incomes which the historical literature refers to. However,

there is one study which does lend some support to this position, although

its results are not conclusive. This is the Reports of the Immigration

Commission, presented to Congress in 1910, although the Commission

was created in 1907.[1] These reports provided much of the basis for the

---

[1]United States Congress, Senate, The Immigration Commission, Abstracts of Reports of the Immigration Commission, I, 61st Congress, 3rd Session, Senate, Document No. 747 (Washington: Government Printing Office, 1911).

restrictive immigration laws of the next decade and as such became quite

controversial. One of the difficulties of using the reports as indicators of

relative economic position of native and foreign born is that the Com-

mission ended up proving what it assumed to be true in the first place.

In the introductory pages of the first volume under the heading: Plan

and Scope of the Inquiry, the following statements are made:

> The old and the new immigration differ in many essentials.
> The former was, from the beginning, largely a movement
> of settlers who came from the most progressive sections
> of Europe for the purpose of making for themselves homes
> in the New World. . . . They mingled freely with the[1]
> native Americans and were quickly assimilated. . . .

> On the other hand, the new immigration has been largely a
> movement of unskilled laboring men who have come, in
> large part temporarily, from the less progressive and ad-
> vanced countries of Europe in response to the call for in-
> dustrial workers in the eastern and middle western
> states. . . .[2]

> The new immigration as a class is far less intelligent than
> the old. . . .[3]

> Consequently the Commission paid little attention to the
> foreign born element of the old immigrant class and
> directed its efforts almost entirely to an inquiry relative
> to the general status of the newer immigrants of the United
> States.[4]

---

[1]United States Congress, Senate, The Immigration Commission, Abstracts of Reports of the Immigration Commission, I, 61st Congress, 3rd Session, Senate, Document No. 747 (Washington: Government Printing Office, 1911), 13.

[2]Ibid., p. 14.

[3]Ibid., p. 14.

[4]Ibid., p. 14.

In view of these quotes it is not surprising that the Commission
has been charged with producing a prejudiced report, which was generally
too favorable to the recent immigrants. However, one cannot dismiss
their findings too easily, and a discussion of their results is in order.
Some 619, 595 employees are included in the study, and most of the data
is concentrated in twenty industries in manufacturing and mining. Most of
the data is based upon various subsamples, but no strong biases in the
sampling methods are evident. Undoubtedly this sample is not representative of the entire immigrant population since it centers on manufacturing,
but the same criticism can be leveled at the other reports cited previously.
One of the tables presents the average amount of weekly earnings of male
employees 18 years of age and over, with all the data apparently based
upon studies made in 1908. A summary of these weekly earnings is presented in Table 18. Only nativity groups representing five per cent or more
of the foreign born population are presented separately in the table.

In this sample there are 220, 390 represented, with 139, 610 of
them being foreign born. This data indicates an economic position of the
foreign born considerably lower than that reported in any previous studies.
Although the old immigrants, the English, German and Irish are still quite
comparable to the native born, they are swamped by the "new immigrants"
with much lower earnings. Two other tables in the Reports make the situation even more difficult to interpret. The average amount of daily earnings of the foreign born male employees 18 and over was 97 per cent of the

native born earnings for the same group. [1] It does not appear that these

estimates are based upon overlapping samples. The weekly earnings

data is compiled from industries where employees were paid on a piece

rate basis, thus "it was found more satisfactory to tabulate the returns

according to the amount earned each week rather than each day."[2] It

also seems the data on daily earnings comes just from industries where

the wage rate was expressed in terms of daily earnings. It is not clear

TABLE 18

WEEKLY EARNINGS, MALES 18 AND OVER[a]

Nativity	Percentage of Foreign Born	Income as a Percentage of Native Born Income
French Canadian	5. 8	76
English	6. 7	102
German	8. 2	98
Irish	5. 4	94
Italian, North	3. 8	81
Italian, South	5. 6	69
Polish	17. 4	80
Slovak	7. 7	86
Total Foreign Born	100. 0	86

[a]U. S. Congress, Abstracts of Reports of the Immigration Commission, p. 367.

[1]Ibid., p. 371.

[2]Ibid., pp. 366-67.

why such a marked difference in earnings would exist for the two esti-

mates. It could be argued that the foreign born who entered the indus-

tries where work was done on a piece-rate basis were of a lower labor

force quality than the foreign born who entered other industries, but it

would seem that the same distribution according to quality would have

existed among the native born workers. Therefore, it seems odd that

with two separate samples, both quite large, one would show immigrant

earnings considerably below those of the native born and the other indi-

cates earnings (or at least wage rates) were quite comparable. The

situation becomes even more complex when one examines the yearly

earnings of males 18 years of age and over. In this case the Immigration

Commission reports native born earnings as $600 and foreign born as

$455, or only 76 per cent of the native born.[1] In this case the sample

is much smaller than in the two previous instances, a total of 26,616

with 22,938 being foreign born.

Although the different samples report somewhat conflicting

conclusions about the relative economic positions of the native and

foreign born for 1908, one cannot dismiss the possibility that the in-

comes of the foreign born were considerably less than those of the native

born. One possible explanation is readily apparent when one examines

the number of immigrants for the period 1870 through 1920 in Table 20

of Appendix A.

[1]Ibid., p. 408.

If earnings were low for an immigrant for the first several years in the country, the very large increase in number of immigrants after the turn of the century could have resulted in low average incomes for all immigrants. The big influx would have meant that a much larger proportion of the foreign born population than previously was relatively new in the country, thus depressing average earnings. This could have happened even apart from national differences between immigrant groups.

Another possible explanation for the Immigrant Commission's results is the differences in the age structure between the foreign born that they sampled and the rest of the foreign born population. It could have been that the recent immigrants, which made up a large portion of the Commission's sample, were largely concentrated in low income earning age groups. Then, even if these immigrants had the same income profile over time as the rest of the foreign born population a sample which contained a large portion of the more recent immigrants would indicate low earnings for the foreign born. Data is not available on the age structure of the various immigrant groups for the year of the Immigration Commission survey, 1908. However, one can approximate the desired information by looking at the age structure of the foreign born in the closest census year, 1910, and comparing it with the age structure of the immigrants who entered in the years just before that date. Age structure is available on the entering immigrants.[1] However, it is

---

[1] Historical Statistics of the United States, Colonial Times to 1957, Series C 133-138, p. 62.

available only for broad categories; under 14 years, 14 to 44 years, and 45 and over. By assuming that the entering immigrants within a category were evenly distributed among all ages in that category for the first two categories, and evenly distributed between 45 and 65 in the last, one can construct an age distribution for the entering population. I have done this for the five years prior to 1910, 1905 through 1909. Then, from this data one can construct an age distribution for 1910 for the immigrants that entered from 1905 through 1909. Using 1890 headship rates and income profile information used earlier one can compute relative earnings of the recent immigrant group and the total foreign born present in 1910.[1] The recent immigrants' earnings would have been 3.8 per cent higher than those of the total foreign born if age structure alone were the only factor influencing income. Therefore it cannot be argued that the relatively low foreign born earnings reported by the Immigration Commission are the result of a sample which was strongly biased towards a group which had low earnings because of its age structure.

Thus there is no strong evidence that disproves the conclusions of the Immigration Commission, that, at least for 1908, the "new immigrants" were of a much lower productivity than the "old." Nevertheless, if the Commission's representation of earning for 1908 is accurate, it seems doubtful that this condition prevailed for long, and it appears

---

[1] The headship rates and income profile data is listed in Tables 8 and 7 on pages 55 and 54 respectively.

more likely that the immigrants advanced at a fairly rapid rate to narrow the discrepancy between their economic position and that of the native born. The index of labor force quality used in Chapter II, λ, shows foreign born workers 93 per cent as productive as native workers in 1920. Although this is the lowest value of this index, it still indicates that the foreign born and native born were fairly close. If this index is valid this means that fairly rapid progress must have been made between the relatively low earnings of 1908 and the fairly comparable position of 1920. Unfortunately, the λ index is not available for 1910. Of course it must be remembered that λ is not an index of the same thing as the figures reported in the Immigration Commission Reports, but nevertheless they both are estimates which throw light upon the question of relative economic position and abilities raised in the historical literature.

Although the Immigration Commission Reports make for less conclusive results, it does seem that, for at least most of the historical period of immigration, the relative skills and economic positions of the native and foreign born were quite comparable. This conclusion, of course, is much at variance with the position taken by most historical authors.

APPENDIX A

TABLES RELATING TO THE NATIVE AND FOREIGN BORN

TABLE 19

NATIVITY GROUP POPULATIONS EXPRESSED IN ABSOLUTE FIGURES
AND AS PERCENTAGE OF TOTAL POPULATION[a]

Population (1000s)

Year	Total Population	Native Born	Foreign Born	Native Born		
				Native Parents	Foreign Parents	Mixed Parents
1850	23,192	20,947	2,245			
1860	31,443	27,305	4,139			
1870	38,558	32,991	5,567	27,666		5,325[b]
1880	50,156	43,476	6,680	35,233	6,332	1,911
1890	62,948	53,698	9,250	42,194	11,504[b]	
1900	75,995	65,653	10,341	49,956	10,651	5,046
1910	91,972	78,456	13,516	59,491	12,949	6,016
1920	105,710	91,790	13,921	68,995	15,764	7,031

Percentage of Total Population

Year		Native Born	Foreign Born	Native Born		
				Native Parents	Foreign Parents	Mixed Parents
1850		90.3	9.7			
1860		86.8	13.2			
1870		85.6	14.4	71.8		13.8[b]
1880		86.7	13.3	70.2	12.6	3.8
1890		85.3	14.7	67.0	18.3[b]	
1900		86.4	13.6	65.7	14.0	6.6
1910		85.3	14.7	64.7	14.1	6.5
1920		86.8	13.2	65.3	14.9	6.6

[a]U. S. Department of Commerce, Bureau of the Census, Fourteenth Census of the United States, 1920, II, 30, Table 4.

[b]For the dates 1870 and 1890 no differentiation is made between the native born of foreign parents and those of mixed parents.

TABLE 22

AGE DISTRIBUTION OF THE NATIVE AND FOREIGN BORN,
1870-1920, EXPRESSED IN PERCENTAGES[a]

	0-19 Years of age	20-49 Years of age	50+ Years of age
1870			
Native Born	56.0	34.2	9.8
Foreign Born	14.3	67.8	18.0
1880			
Native Born	44.4	36.6	19.0
Foreign Born	12.3	63.4	24.3
1890			
Native Born	51.2	38.3	10.5
Native Parents	48.0	38.9	13.1
Foreign or Mixed Parents	54.1	41.5	4.5
Foreign Born	10.5	60.4	29.1
1900			
Native Born	49.4	39.5	11.0
Native Parents	47.6	38.7	13.6
Foreign or Mixed Parents	54.1	41.5	4.5
Foreign Born	10.5	60.4	29.1
1910			
Native Born	47.3	40.5	12.2
Native Parents	46.1	40.0	13.9
Foreign or Mixed Parents	50.0	42.0	8.0
Foreign Born	10.7	63.5	26.0
1920			
Native Born	45.6	40.6	13.4
Native Parents	45.2	40.6	14.0
Foreign or Mixed Parents	47.1	41.3	11.5
Foreign Born	7.8	62.0	30.1

[a]Sources: 1870: U. S. Department of Commerce, Bureau of the Census, Ninth Census of the United States, 1870, II, Vital Statistics, 552. 1880 and 1890: U. S. Department of Commerce, Bureau of the Census, Eleventh Census of the United States, 1890, Compendium 3, p. 190. 1900-1920: U. S. Department of Commerce, Bureau of the Census, Fourteenth Census of the United States, 1920, II, 160, Table 7.

TABLE 23

LABOR FORCE PARTICIPATION RATES BY AGE, 1890[a]

Age	Native White Native Parents		Native White, Foreign or Mixed Parents		Foreign Born	
	Male %	Female %	Male %	Female %	Male %	Female %
10 to 14	7.4	2.5	7.5	3.7	15.6	9.8
15 to 19	49.4	15.8	63.8	33.7	81.7	58.8
20 to 24	89.2	19.9	92.6	36.6	96.6	45.4
25 to 34	97.1	11.4	97.2	19.2	98.3	19.8
35 to 44	97.6	9.2	97.7	12.1	98.3	12.0
45 to 54	96.2	9.8	95.4	10.9	97.0	10.5
55 to 64	93.1	9.9	91.6	10.7	91.4	9.4
65+	74.2	6.7	71.7	7.2	69.0	6.1
Age Unknown	69.2	22.2	73.3	31.1	90.0	37.6

[a]Source: U. S. Department of Commerce, Bureau of the Census, Eleventh Census of United States, 1890, Population, Part 2, p. cxxii.

TABLE 24

OCCUPATIONAL DISTRIBUTION OF THE NATIVE
AND FOREIGN BORN, 1880-1890[a]

	1880 (%)		1890 (%)	
	Native Born	Foreign Born	Native Born	Foreign Born
Agriculture, Fisheries, and Mining	50. 6	27. 8	43. 9	25. 5
Professional Service	3. 8	2. 1	4. 7	2. 2
Domestic and Personal Service	18. 2	27. 7	16. 7	27. 6
Trade and Transportation	10. 3	12. 6	40. 8	13. 9
Manufacturing and Mechanical Industries	17. 1	29. 8	19. 9	30. 9

[a]Source: U. S. Department of Commerce, Bureau of the Census, Eleventh Census of the United States, Population, Part 2, p. cxlviii.

APPENDIX B

DERIVATION OF ESTIMATES OF LABOR FORCE QUALITY

The estimates of λ presented in Table 1 of the thesis are an
important part of my work. There has been considerable speculation
about the relative quality of the native and foreign born labor forces,
but to my knowledge, no estimates have been made of these quality
differences. My estimates follow the method used by Gary Becker in
determining the relative occupational position of Negroes and whites in
his The Economics of Discrimination.[1] Becker classified all Negro
and white workers into three skill categories, skilled, semi-skilled,
and unskilled, and then weighted these by the relative wages of the three
categories. Since relative wage information for these categories is not
available for the nineteenth century, I have used the same relative wage
estimates as Becker. His estimates are taken from Morton Zeman, A
Quantitative Analysis of White-Non-White Income Differentials in the
United States in 1939.[2] These estimates are based on income received
by whites in 1940 and are given for two regions, the North and the South.
The relative position of skilled, semi-skilled, and unskilled occupations
is represented by 2.34, 1.44, and 1.00 in the North, and by 2.69, 1.49,
and 1.00 for the South.[3] Since I am concerned with the relative

---

[1]Gary S. Becker, The Economics of Discrimination (Chicago:
The University of Chicago Press, 1957), p. 113.

[2]Morton Zeman, "A Quantitative Analysis of White-Non-White
Income Differentials in the United States in 1939" (unpublished Ph. D.
dissertation, Department of Economics, University of Chicago, 1955),
Appendix D.

[3]Becker, The Economics of Discrimination, p. 113.

occupational positions for the entire United States, I have weighted the estimates for the North and the South by the percentage of the total labor force in each region for each of the years under consideration. This yielded the results of Table 25.

TABLE 25

RELATIVE WAGES OF SKILL CATEGORIES, 1870-1920

	1870	1880	1890	1900	1910	1920
Skilled	2.445	2.446	2.439	2.442	2.446	2.436
Semi-Skilled	1.455	1.455	1.454	1.455	1.454	1.454
Unskilled	1.000	1.000	1.000	1.000	1.000	1.000

Since these estimates are all very close, I chose to use 2.44, 1.45, and 1.00 for the entire period, rather than use the separate, slightly more precise figures for each census date.

In order to properly classify the native and foreign born labor force into the three categories, I used a 1937 Bureau of Census classification system which lists alphabetically each specific occupation and assigns each occupation to one of eight "social-economic groups."[1] The

[1]Alba M. Edwards, Alphabetical Index of Occupations by Industries and Social-Economic Classes, United States Department of Commerce, Bureau of the Census (Washington: Government Printing Office, 1937).

eight groups and my corresponding skill classifications are:

> Skilled
>> Professional persons
>> Farmers (owners and tenants)
>> Proprietors, managers and officials (except farmers)
>> Clerks and kindred workers
>> Skilled workers and foremen
>
> Semi-skilled
>> Semi-skilled workers (mostly factory operatives)
>
> Unskilled
>> Farm laborers
>> Other laborers
>> Servant classes

This classification system corresponds quite closely to the one used by Becker in constructing his estimates from Zeman's data, since he states:

> The average wage and salary income of white professional workers, proprietors and officials, clerical and sales workers, and foremen and craftsmen was used as the average income of skilled whites; the wage and salary income of white operatives as the income of semi-skilled whites; and the wage and salary income of white laborers as the income of unskilled whites. [1]

The relative occupational positions arrived at through the application of this classification system are presented in Table 26 below. It should be noted that the relative number of native and foreign born in each category is based upon the total number engaged in occupations that could be classified. In each census year there was a certain number of occupations that could not be classified, either because the

---

[1] Becker, The Economics of Discrimination, p. 113, footnote 4.

occupation did not exist in 1937, or, more often, because the census category was too broad, e.g., railroad employees. The percentage of the total labor force that was unclassifiable is listed below.

1870	1880	1890	1900	1920
1.8%	2.8%	3.0%	4.0%	0.1%

The number of occupations varied considerably over the period. The number for each census year is presented in the next tabulation.

1870	1880	1890	1900	1920
338	265	224	140	580

TABLE 26

THE PERCENTAGE OF NATIVE AND FOREIGN BORN
IN SKILL CATEGORIES[a]

Year	% Skilled		% Semi-Skilled		% Unskilled	
	Native Born	Foreign Born	Native Born	Foreign Born	Native Born	Foreign Born
1870	43.0	36.6	12.7	23.2	44.3	40.2
1880	43.1	38.6	14.6	25.4	42.2	36.0
1890	49.4	40.5	17.3	25.0	33.3	34.5
1900	45.8	39.5	17.6	26.7	36.6	33.8
1910	(b)	41.9	(b)	23.8	(b)	34.3
1920	56.1	44.6	15.9	23.8	28.0	32.2

TABLE 26--Continued

---

[a]Calculated from U. S. Department of Commerce, Bureau of
Census, Censuses from 1870 through 1920. 1870: Ninth Census of the
United States, 1870, I, Population, 704-714, Table 29. 1880: Tenth
Census of the United States, 1880, I, Population, 744-750, Table 27.
1890: Eleventh Census of the United States, 1890, XII, Population,
Part 2, 354-358, Table 82. 1900: Twelfth Census of the United States,
1900, Special Reports, Occupations, pp. 10-12, Table 2. 1920:
Fourteenth Census of the United States, IV, Population, 342-359, Table
5. 1910: E. P. Hutchinson, Immigrants and Their Children, 1850-
1950 (New York: John Wiley, 1956), pp. 204-206, Table 39.

[b]Estimates for the total population are not available for 1910,
although data does exist for the native white population. An estimate
based upon this data is discussed later.

Application of Becker's weights to the data of Table 26 yields

the relative occupational positions of Table 27. Contrary to the opinions

expressed in most of the literature, there seems to have been very little

difference in the quality of the native and foreign born labor forces.

Also, no definite trend is evident in these estimates, although most

writers seemed to feel that the later immigrants were of much lower

quality than the earlier ones.

The 1910 census does not allow a comparison between the total

native born labor force and the foreign born, but this comparison can

be made between the native white and the foreign born. A comparison

between the native white and the foreign born was also made for 1890.

The results are presented below in Table 28.

TABLE 27

INDICES OF RELATIVE OCCUPATIONAL POSITIONS

	1870	1880	1890	1900	1920
Native Born	1.68	1.69	1.79	1.74	1.88
Foreign Born	1.63	1.67	1.70	1.69	1.75
$\lambda = \dfrac{\text{Foreign Born}}{\text{Native Born}}$	.97	.99	.95	.97	.93

TABLE 28

INDICES OF RELATIVE OCCUPATIONAL POSITIONS,
NATIVE WHITE AND FOREIGN BORN[a]

	1890	1910
Native White	1.87	1.88
Foreign Born	1.70	1.71
$\lambda = \dfrac{\text{Foreign Born}}{\text{Native Born}}$	.91	.91

[a]Calculated from: 1890: U. S. Department of Commerce, Bureau of the Census, Eleventh Census of the United States, XII, Population, Part 2, 354-358, Table 82. 1910: E. P. Hutchinson, Immigrants and Their Children, 1850-1950 (New York: John Wiley, 1956), pp. 204-206, Table 39.

The data of Tables 27 and 28 is quite surprising since it indicates

a relatively close economic position of the native and foreign born. Even

when the colored population is excluded from the native population, as in

Table 28, the foreign born are still 90 per cent as productive as the

native white. A major problem with these results, however, may lie in

the application of 1940 relative wage data to the nineteenth century occu-

pational distribution figures. Relative wages for unskilled, semi-

skilled, and skilled have undoubtedly changed through time, and this

could bias my results. To check the sensitivity of my results to changes

in relative wages I have recomputed λ for one of the years, 1870, using

several different sets of relative wages. These are chosen so as to

bracket by a fairly large margin the possible changes in relative wages

that could have occurred. Table 29 presents the sets of values for rela-

tive wages that are used as alternatives to the 2.44, 1.45, and 1.00 used

previously. It also lists λ for each of these alternative sets.

TABLE 29

INDICES OF RELATIVE OCCUPATIONAL POSITIONS USING
HYPOTHETICAL RELATIVE WAGES, 1870

Skill Category	Relative Wages	λ	Relative Wages	λ	Relative Wages	λ
Skilled	2.0		3.0		3.0	
Semi-Skilled	1.2	.98	2.0	.99	1.2	.94
Unskilled	1.0		1.0		1.0	

Thus it is clear that the use of 1940 wage data does not seriously bias my results. Use of any plausible values for relative wages yields estimates of relative labor force quality of the native and foreign born that are quite close. Contrary to popular supposition, the native and foreign born differed little in skill levels and economic position.

Dissertations in American Economic History

An Arno Press Collection

Adams, Donald R., Jr. **Wage Rates in Philadelphia, 1790-1830.**
(Doctoral Dissertation, University of Pennsylvania, 1967). 1975

Aldrich, Terry Mark. **Rates of Return on Investment in Technical
Education in the Ante-Bellum American Economy.** (Doctoral
Dissertation, The University of Texas at Austin, 1969). 1975

Anderson, Terry Lee. **The Economic Growth of Seventeenth
Century New England:** A Measurement of Regional Income.
(Doctoral Dissertation, University of Washington, 1972). 1975

Bean, Richard Nelson. **The British Trans-Atlantic Slave Trade,
1650-1775.** (Doctoral Dissertation, University of Washington,
1971). 1975

Brock, Leslie V. **The Currency of the American Colonies,
1700-1764:** A Study in Colonial Finance and Imperial Relations.
(Doctoral Dissertation, University of Michigan, 1941). 1975

Ellsworth, Lucius F. **Craft to National Industry in the Nineteenth
Century:** A Case Study of the Transformation of the New York
State Tanning Industry. (Doctoral Dissertation, University of
Delaware, 1971). 1975

Fleisig, Heywood W. **Long Term Capital Flows and the Great
Depression:** The Role of the United States, 1927-1933.
(Doctoral Dissertation, Yale University, 1969). 1975

Foust, James D. **The Yeoman Farmer and Westward Expansion
of U. S. Cotton Production.** (Doctoral Dissertation, University of
North Carolina at Chapel Hill, 1968). 1975

Golden, James Reed. **Investment Behavior By United States
Railroads, 1870-1914.** (Doctoral Thesis, Harvard University,
1971). 1975

Hill, Peter Jensen. **The Economic Impact of Immigration into the
United States.** (Doctoral Dissertation, The University of Chicago,
1970). 1975

Klingaman, David C. **Colonial Virginia's Coastwise and Grain
Trade.** (Doctoral Dissertation, University of Virginia, 1967). 1975

Lang, Edith Mae. **The Effects of Net Interregional Migration on
Agricultural Income Growth:** The United States, 1850-1860.
(Doctoral Thesis, The University of Rochester, 1971). 1975

Lindley, Lester G. **The Constitution Faces Technology:**
The Relationship of the National Government to the Telegraph,
1866-1884. (Doctoral Thesis, Rice University, 1971). 1975

Lorant, John H[erman]. **The Role of Capital-Improving
Innovations in American Manufacturing During the 1920's.**
(Doctoral Thesis, Columbia University, 1966). 1975

Mishkin, David Joel. **The American Colonial Wine Industry:** An Economic Interpretation, Volumes I and II. (Doctoral Thesis, University of Illinois, 1966). 1975

Oates, Mary J. **The Role of the Cotton Textile Industry in the Economic Development of the American Southeast:** 1900-1940. (Doctoral Dissertation, Yale University, 1969). 1975

Passell, Peter. **Essays in the Economics of Nineteenth Century American Land Policy.** (Doctoral Dissertation, Yale University, 1970). 1975

Pope, Clayne L. **The Impact of the Ante-Bellum Tariff on Income Distribution.** (Doctoral Dissertation, The University of Chicago, 1972). 1975

Poulson, Barry Warren. **Value Added in Manufacturing, Mining, and Agriculture in the American Economy From 1809 To 1839.** (Doctoral Dissertation, The Ohio State University, 1965). 1975

Rockoff, Hugh. **The Free Banking Era: A Re-Examination.** (Doctoral Dissertation, The University of Chicago, 1972). 1975

Schumacher, Max George. **The Northern Farmer and His Markets During the Late Colonial Period.** (Doctoral Dissertation, University of California at Berkeley, 1948). 1975

Seagrave, Charles Edwin. **The Southern Negro Agricultural Worker:** 1850-1870. (Doctoral Dissertation, Stanford University, 1971). 1975

Solmon, Lewis C. **Capital Formation by Expenditures on Formal Education, 1880 and 1890.** (Doctoral Dissertation, The University of Chicago, 1968). 1975

Swan, Dale Evans. **The Structure and Profitability of the Antebellum Rice Industry:** 1859. (Doctoral Dissertation, University of North Carolina at Chapel Hill, 1972). 1975

Sylla, Richard Eugene. **The American Capital Market, 1846-1914:** A Study of the Effects of Public Policy on Economic Development. (Doctoral Thesis, Harvard University, 1968) 1975

Uselding, Paul John. **Studies in the Technological Development of the American Economy During the First Half of the Nineteenth Century.** (Doctoral Dissertation, Northwestern University, 1970) 1975

Walsh, William D[avid]. **The Diffusion of Technological Change in the Pennsylvania Pig Iron Industry, 1850-1870.** (Doctoral Dissertation, Yale University, 1967). 1975

Weiss, Thomas Joseph. **The Service Sector in the United States, 1839 Through 1899.** (Doctoral Thesis, University of North Carolina at Chapel Hill, 1967). 1975

Zevin, Robert Brooke. **The Growth of Manufacturing in Early Nineteenth Century New England.** 1975